D1477293

# The
# Photographic
# Kama Sutra

# The Photographic Kama Sutra

Exotic positions inspired by the classic Indian text

## Linda Sonntag

hamlyn

First published in Great Britain in 2001 by Hamlyn,
a division of Octopus Publishing Group Limited,
2–4 Heron Quays, Docklands, London, E14 4JP.

Copyright © 2001 Octopus Publishing Group Limited

All rights reserved. No part of this publication may be
reproduced stored in a retrieval system or transmitted
in any form, or by any means, electronic, mechanical,
photocopying or otherwise without the prior permission
of the publisher.

ISBN 0 600 60234 6

A CIP catalogue record of this book is available
from the British Library.

Printed in Hong Kong
The author has asserted her moral rights

# WARNING

With the prevalence of AIDS and other sexually transmitted
diseases, if you do not practise safe sex you are risking
your life and your partner's life.

# Contents

**Right:** The imagination of Indian artists has no bounds. In this impossibly exotic configuration, sexual acrobats explore the delights of fantasy.

# Introduction

In ancient India, as elsewhere in the ancient world, sex was celebrated and explored without shame. Sometime between the first and fourth centuries AD in Benares, a holy sage called Vatsyayana, about whom little else is known, wrote down everything he could discover about the sexual practices of his countryfolk in a meticulous guide to sexual etiquette called the Kama Sutra. His work is more a treatise than a pillow book – its title translates as 'the science of pleasure'. The sage dedicated his researches to the goddess from whom all ecstasy flows. The Kama Sutra mirrors the privileged world that Vatsyayana inhabited, a world saturated with indolence, luxury and intrigue. The objective of upper class Indian society was the pursuit of pleasure, and its obsessions were seduction and sex. Amoral and materialistic as this world was, it also reached a spiritual dimension, and sex was the gateway to achieving it.

Experiences that transcend time and place bring a deep happiness and fulfilment that put everyday problems into perspective. They enable us to tap into a well of generosity and deal lightly and kindly with the world. Emotionally committed sex provides one way of experiencing the transcendant. The ancient Indian sages found that yoga provides another. Yoga and sex together form the basis of tantrism, or spiritual sex. Yoga means literally 'yoke' - it is said to have been invented by the god Shiva, Lord of the Dance, to join himself in sex to the fundamental creative power of the ultimate goddess, Kali. The Tantrists believed that women possess more spiritual energy than men, and that men could join themselves to the divinity only through sacred, highly charged emotional sex with a woman.

The love positions presented in original photographic sequences in *The Photographic Kama Sutra* and depicted in the exquisite Indian miniatures featured in the book have all been inspired by yoga. For some of the sequences in this book, the lovers need to be strong, graceful and supple. Practice in yoga will benefit all the poses, as well as enhancing your self-awareness, increasing your vitality and improving your ability to relax. Introduce yourselves gradually to the poses, use them as inspiration for your own sexual journey and avoid forcing anything that does not come naturally. May the goddess be with you!

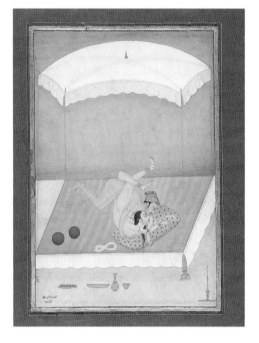

**Above:** Yoga practice gave the lovers of ancient India strong and supple bodies. Nevertheless, it is difficult to believe that some of the love poses depicted in these miniatures could ever be achieved.

Centre Yourself

# The Head

The head is the closest part of the body to heaven, and the way you hold your head shows how you feel about yourself in relation to heaven. Learn to hold your head like a dancer. Stand in your bare feet, and feel their connection to the ground. Now bring your mind up your body to your pelvis. Imagine it as a dish of water. Feel your spine growing upwards from this dish like a plant shooting towards the Sun. Imagine a flower blooming at the top of the stem: this is how you should hold your head.

The women of the East who carry water jars on their heads move with grace and dignity. Imagine you are carrying life-giving water from the well in a clay pot made in your own kiln. Feel your head centred above your belly as you glide forwards against the blue sky, walking so your toes make contact with the sandy road before your heels. You are learning your body all over again through walking with sensual awareness. When you stoop to pick up a bangle that has slipped from your wrist, watch it glinting from the corner of your eye and bend from the knees to keep your water jar balanced on your head. This is an exercise you can practise anywhere, any time.

Because the hair springs from the head, it is thought to be the dwelling place of the soul. It concentrates its owner's personality, vitality and sexuality and has magic powers as a love charm. Lovers all over the world and throughout history have exchanged locks of hair as pledges. In some cultures the hair of a bride and groom are shampooed in the same basin at their wedding, then their hair is twisted together into one strand to unite the pair for life. The same idea lies behind braiding dances, often seen embroidered and appliquéd on Indian wedding cloths. The men move sunwise or clockwise and the women dance in the opposite direction, moonwise, so that the sexes are woven together. In the maypole dance, the ribbons stand in for the rays of the Sun and the Moon and also for hair braided as a fertility charm.

**Above:** For a woman, grooming and adorning herself for love can be a delightful build-up to erotic relaxation.

## The hair, the gods and sexual energy

Tantric sages believed that women could activate forces of creation and destruction by binding and unbinding their hair. The goddess Kali unleashed violent thunderstorms by freeing her long tresses into wildly writhing serpents, and calmed the skies again by combing them. Her partner Shiva is a hairy god – his unruly locks represent the creative and sexual energy of the universe and must on no account be cut, or he would be castrated like Samson. Even to this day Indian men keep their hair long and wrapped in a turban to preserve its vital essences.

Students of the Kama Sutra learned the arts of beautifying their hair by colouring it with henna, dressing it with perfumes and unguents, making braids, chaplets, turbans, crests and topknots of flowers. While the hair on the head was celebrated, men shaved their beards and both sexes removed all body hair. If a wealthy courtesan wanted to assess a potential new client, she would send shampooers, singers and jesters to his house. The shampooers would rub the man's body as well as his hair. If she liked what she heard, the courtesan might then seduce him with an erotic hair dance, in which her hair was rubbed with perfumed oils then swung loose with passionate movements of her head.

*Below:* Damp with sweat and hanging free, a woman's hair is more beautiful during love-making than after a session with the most talented stylist.

# The Eyes

**Below:** The lovers read each other's character and wishes through deep, silent, constant eye-contact.

Your eyes are worlds of feeling distilled into colour and light. They bring messages direct from your soul, unedited by thought processes, faster, deeper, truer, more subtle and fleeting than words. The first sparks of instant sexuality pass unconsciously through the eloquence of the eyes. Later, they become a channel of desire – one glance can set two bodies on fire, and in the conflagration that follows, the naked power of the eyes fixes the act of love in eternity.

Some people train themselves to hide the feeling in their eyes. Thereby they lose beauty and character and become less true to themselves. Real eye contact takes courage – you reveal vulnerability as well as strength, and it is easy to get swept away on diving into the eyes of another. Take your time. When you are overwhelmed, remember that seeing is a two-way process – you are giving power as well as receiving it.

Of course, for most of its waking life the eye does not transmit intense emotion. It is cool rather than warm, the organ through which we perceive the world around us. The eye stands for intellectual perception – 'I see' means 'I understand'. The eye is a judge that discerns, distinguishes – and condemns.

## The evil eye

Because of its power of condemnation, the evil eye strikes terror into those it watches. The people of ancient India used yonic symbols (symbols of the vulva) to protect themselves against the evil eye. A cowrie shell was a most effective amulet that could be carried about a person or worn as a necklace, but even a simple triangle daubed on the door of the house would do. Still today in northern India farmers protect their crops by hanging Kali's black pot, a symbol of the goddess's vagina, in their fields.

In ancient India the two eyes were identified with the Sun and the Moon. The right eye belonged to the Sun and was concerned with actions and the future; the left eye was a child of the Moon, linked to the passive and the past. To resolve this duality was the

**Left and below:** The brain is the body's most important sex organ. It gives and receives messages of desire through the eyes.

function of the third eye, the eye in Shiva's forehead. Our eyes create a distance between us and what we look at; they observe limits, defining the world which is not the self. But our inner eye – the third eye – destroys boundaries, it unites and synthesizes. This is the eye of the heart and the recipient of spiritual enlightenment. To reach the vision of your inner eye is to see and understand yourself.

## The inner eye

The inner eye is the place where revelations occur. These often happen in that mysterious dreamworld between waking and sleeping. Who has not mulled over a problem for days without making progress, only to have the answer leap up fully fledged at the moment of waking? Train yourself to hover on the verge of consciousness, and stay in this colourful fluid zone where you will discover your most creative thoughts and feelings. Try doing this with your partner as you fall asleep together, and share your dreams and visions when you wake up.

To throw off staleness or release stress and revive yourself after a wearing day, lie down and close your eyes. Relax, breathing deeply. Focus your attention on the place where your third eye is situated – just above and between your eyebrows. Let it fill with coloured light and roll out a bright carpet before you. Now step out on to it and imagine you are in a magical forest where the laws and limitations of the everyday world have been suspended and you can be entirely yourself for as long as you like. Allow yourself to wander freely in the wildness of your imagination. When you wish to return, roll in the carpet and focus your attention again on your third eye. Lie still for a few moments before rejoining the world outside.

# The Ears

Our ears provide us with the longest living of all our senses. When the body is on its deathbed and can no longer feel, taste, smell or see, it can still recognize the voices of those it has loved. The sense of hearing is also the first to develop – the inner ear begins to form as early as the seventh day after conception, and by four and a half months, it has reached its final size. The newborn baby has considerable experience of the world of sound. For nine months it has listened to its mother's heartbeat and a constant symphony of bloopings, rumblings and gurglings.

**Below:** Listening to the music of nature brings peace, power and a sense of oneness with the universe.

## Music

Our heartbeat is the rhythm of life; it measures every moment until our last and places us firmly at the centre of our own universe. The first sounds – the beat of the heart, the melodic rushings inside the womb – are the beginnings of music. Music transports the soul through a vast range of emotions, from sadness and pain to exultation. With our ears full of music, we are carried back to that blissful state when we were protected from all harm, had no responsibility and perceived the world only as sound.

From the beginning music was at the heart of religious life; it celebrated, commemorated and mourned each coming and going. Today at the touch of a button we can call on musicians from around the world to play in our homes and bring us healing, dissolve blockages, lift our spirits and drift us back into memory.

The music of the West is built on time, but the music of the East is composed of repeating melodies that spiral into eternity. To centre yourself, listen to the music of eternity. Hang wind chimes in a tree by your window, close your eyes when rain beats on the roof, lose yourself in the howling of the wind and the crashing of the waves. Hold a shell to your ear. Do you hear the roar of the ocean or is it the tumult of your own heart? They are one and the same. One spring dawn, record the birdsong in your garden. Then play it back on winter mornings when you get up in the dark to remind you of what is to come.

# Words of love

Remember that the inner ear is also the organ of balance. And as befits an organ whose job is to keep us upright, the ear is objective. Sound waves – vibrations in the air – are funnelled by the outer ear to the inner ear, then taken as electrical signals to the brain, where they are interpreted as sound. This precise process gives us understanding of language. Thus the ear is crucial in the formation of the questions and answers on which all human relationships are built, and in the development of our spiritual and mental faculties.

The ear is a receptacle. When a man speaks words of love, they pour like warm honey into the ear of a woman just as his sperm shoots into her vagina. It takes words as well as sperm to find a fertile womb. In the Christian religion, the word of God took the role of sperm when it entered Mary's ear through the angel Gabriel and she conceived his son.

Your ears take in so much information all day long that the time comes to unplug and free yourself from the residue of it all, the babble of nonsense that still blares inside your head. Teach yourself to empty your head and listen to the silence and be silent with your partner. It is a skill worth learning, to trick the indefatigable brain into switching off so we can commune with ourselves in silence. All sound aims to return to the silence from which it sprang.

**Left:** Shiva and his consort entertain friends with music and song. In ancient India music was often the prelude to love.

# The Nose

Breath is the symbol of life; amongst its blessings are inspiration and understanding. The nose through which we breathe is associated with intuition, the mysterious sixth sense that is illogical but uncannily right. In ancient rites, the magic powders used in making contact with spirits and unseen forces were prepared from the noses and snouts of wild animals.

The average human nose can detect around 4,000 different smells, each one bringing its own message. Invisible and yet very real, scents such as the perfume of a rose, the smell of your lover's sweat or the aroma of a delicious meal make experience vivid and fix us firmly in the present. Scents are also the food of memory, bringing back past scenes and sensations with a sudden wave or jolt of emotion. Scents are so closely related to feelings that the ancient Indians regarded the sense of smell as the most spiritual of all the senses. Perfume, distilled from essences of healing, mood-enhancing plants, stood for purity, and was used liberally to anoint the body for the sacred rites of sex. In temples, it was burned as incense to please the gods. At funerals, it was burned and used in embalming to remember the dead and to purify them for the next life. The essential oils of plants were also important to the yogis. Each perfume symbolized a degree of spiritual perfection; the highest yogis smelled of lotus blossoms.

*Below:* In a private moment after a night of passion, a woman offers her lover a sweetly scented rose. Its perfume brings back a memory of the garden where they first met.

## Breath control

Breath is life, but we pay very little attention to breathing. Most people breathe shallowly through the mouth and hardly use the diaphragm at all. In this way, only a small amount of oxygen is taken into the lungs and only the top of the lungs is used. The lungs are never thoroughly aired and the result is low vitality and low resistance to disease. Good breathing practice will fill the blood with life-giving oxygen to refresh the brain. It will control prana or vital energy, which leads to a balanced and harmonious state of mind. When you are agitated, your breathing is shallow, rapid and irregular. When you are relaxed or deep in thought your breathing is slow and measured. By controlling your breathing

**Above:** Alternate nostril breathing helps to clear the head and lungs. Inhaling the perfume of your partner's skin is one of the greatest pleasures of love.

you can control your state of mind and prepare yourself for concentration and meditation.

The science of breath control is called pranayama, a series of exercises that keeps the body in vibrant health. Breathe through your nose with your mouth closed, so air that enters your lungs is warm and filtered. Above all, breathe deeply to exercise the whole of the lungs. Exhalation is the key to good breathing, for the more stale air you expel from the lungs, the more fresh air you can take in. When you exhale, the abdomen contracts and the diaphragm moves up, massaging the heart; when you inhale, the abdomen expands and the diaphragm moves down, massaging the abdominal organs.

Practise breathing sitting down with your spine, neck and head all in the same line. Try this exercise to get rid of stale air. Inhale gently and deeply, retaining your breath for four counts, then exhale forcefully. Do this twenty times. Alternate nostril breathing is another way of clearing the system. Breathe in through the left nostril, closing the right one with your thumb. Hold your breath, closing both nostrils. Breathe out through the right nostril, closing the left with your fingers. Then breathe in through the right nostril. Repeat the pattern. For a final exercise, try sipping the air. Stick out your tongue and curl the sides up, making a pipe through which to sip the air as you inhale. Close your mouth while you hold your breath, then exhale through the nose.

# The Mouth

*Below and bottom:* The lovers of ancient India perfumed their breath with scented seeds. Fruit offers luscious refreshment between bouts.

Like perfumes, flavours are elusive and impossible to define. Biologists tell us that the tongue is divided into areas that appreciate just four basic tastes: sour, sweet, salty and bitter. But the world of taste is as rich and full of subtlety as the world of colour, and influenced as much by emotion, circumstances and memory as it is by the chemical reaction in the mouth.

The sensual pleasures of eating and drinking are heightened when they are a prelude to love. Food tastes so much more vivid when it's shared, and better still in fresh air – lush grass, birdsong, and strawberries passed in a laughing struggle mouth to mouth. Food for love should be inviting, a captivating arrangement spread simply on a white cloth, colourful, fresh, surprising, and all the better if it needs to be eaten with the fingers, as in India. Salty, fishy tastes, sweet juices that squirt and stream, a rough nutty loaf, thick creams, rich and smooth, that comfort and nourish, sharp sparkling wines that tingle on the tongue and whisk the breath away – all stimulate the palate for the feast that is to follow, the ultimate taste sensations of your lover's skin, mouth and intimate secretions.

The lovers of ancient India paid a great deal of attention to the pleasures of the mouth. The daily toilette included dental hygiene, and sometimes the teeth were blackened for cosmetic effect. The mouth was stimulated prior to lovemaking by singing, laughter and amusing conversation, the drinking of fruit cordials and alcoholic beverages and the eating of delicate sweetmeats. Once their companions had withdrawn for the night, the lovers used their mouths on each other in a complex ritual of kissing and biting, and refreshed themselves between bouts with ripe fruits from the garden. After sex they chewed perfumed seeds to freshen the mouth, and betel nuts wrapped in betel leaves, which give a warm, pleasantly numbing sensation. They also shared a hubble-bubble water pipe or hookah to smoke intoxicating drugs, such as cannabis and magic mushrooms, which were first consecrated to the gods. Like sex itself, these pleasures formed a sacred part of worship.

## The tongue

At the moment of orgasm during mating with Shiva, the goddess Kali (according to the artists who painted her) stuck out her tongue. The Latin word for tongue, lingus, comes from the Sanskrit for phallus, lingam, and gives us our word language, which we also call tongue. To poke the tongue out between the lips was once a sacred gesture representing the lingam in the yoni, and still today the folds of the vulva are called the labiae, lips. In the West, to stick out your tongue at someone is an insult, but in the East, where sex is not linked with shame or disgrace, sticking out the tongue is a polite greeting.

# The Arms and Hands

**_Below and bottom:_** Meeting in a pleasure grove, the lovers entwine arms and hands. The hands especially are eloquent in the language of love.

After the face, the arms and hands are the most expressive parts of our body. We use them in conversation, in wordless contact and in dance to convey a rich range of emotions, both positive and negative. Acceptance and rejection, welcome and threat, happiness and sorrow, triumph and defeat can all be conveyed in a universal language of simple gestures. All over the world, the arms are raised above the head to signify surrender and hopelessness. The hands are used to bless and to curse, and the laying on of hands effects a transfer of energy or power.

Arms stand for strength, power, help and protection, and are also the instruments of justice. The Indian god Brahma is pictured with four faces and four arms to show that he is omnipresent and all-powerful. Ganesh, the elephant-headed god of knowledge, has four arms to symbolize his diversity, and Shiva's countless arms whirl about him as he dances.

The Hindus have a special language of the hands. Fearlessness is expressed by a raised hand, palm forwards and fingers extended. To denote giving, the hand is pointed downwards, palm up, with fingers extending. A clenched fist with the index finger pointing upwards is a threat. Hands join and fold together in a gesture of adoration and prayer, and for meditation the hands rest palms-up on the knees.

## Snake dance

Supple, graceful arms and hands can best express your feelings. The snake dance will help you free them up. Stand comfortably upright with the palms of your hands facing towards the floor. Start the movement with a gentle shake of your shoulders as if you were unfurling laundry in the wind. Let the movement roll down your arms so they flow as though they were boneless. This will

free your shoulders of tension and leave them warm and tingling. Open your chest. Lift up your arms and let them find their own level and rhythm, as if they were being blown by the wind. Let go, fill your lungs with air and let your whole body become energized.

## Giving is the mother of receiving

The first physical contact we make with each other is usually with our hands. When two people are sensitive to one another, a simple touch can convey a world of meaning. People in a close relationship build up a whole vocabulary of touch. Be conscious of the emotions you are transferring to your partner with your hands, such as warmth, confidence, strength, vulnerability, caution, encouragement, desire.

Massage provides a sensual opportunity for wordless communication. Warm the oil in your hands before you begin, then keep the pressure firm and gentle as you move your hands over your lover's body, using fluid strokes that merge into one another. Don't break contact or make any sudden moves that might startle. Follow your instincts, not a sequence from a book. Concentrate on the immediacy and uniqueness of the sensation of touch rather than planning your next move. As you work each area, close your eyes and really learn the body under your hands. Understand the texture of the flesh, the shape and direction of muscles, sinews, bones. Close your eyes and really feel. Work gently on tightened areas to free the tension. For the one who is massaged, your touch becomes their only connection with the world. As the sensations grow more intense, you exist only in the contact between your two bodies. Then let the massage move on, becoming like a dance, like water flowing over stones or the wind blowing through a field of corn. You will find you are receiving as well as giving. Afterwards, lie down side by side and sleep.

*Above left and left:* We use our hands in dance and worship, and to groom, comfort and caress our own bodies as well as to give love.

# The Breasts

The breast is the source of the baby's first nourishment, the milk of human kindness. Breasts stand for comfort, compassion, security and plenty, intimacy and protection. They are also powerful sexual symbols. 'In our maturer years,' wrote Darwin, 'when an object of vision is presented to us which bears any similitude to the form of the female bosom . . . we feel a general glow of delight which seems to influence all our senses, and if the object be not too large we experience an attraction to embrace it with our lips as we did in early infancy the bosom of our mothers.' Only one third of the breast tissue is concerned with milk production. The firm rounded shape has everything to do with sexual signalling. Yet the two functions, to attract and to feed, are inextricably meshed in the mind. A fascinating piece of research into the behaviour of American soldiers in the Vietnam War showed that the closer they were to the battle zone, the more bare-breasted pin-ups they displayed – and the more milk they drank. In a life-threatening situation, the GIs craved a return through sex to the safety of their mother's breast.

Bosom friends, the bosom of the family, returning to the bosom of the earth, all these phrases show the strong connection between the chest, which houses the heart, and a feeling of origin and end, home and belonging. To cuddle close and lay your head on your partner's chest in a secure embrace is a potent antidote to worry and stress. It's a taste and a memory of the unconditional love in which we imagine we basked as babies. In holding and being held and loved we relax and revive into a stronger sense of self.

The breasts extend from the second to the sixth rib and are composed of milk glands encased in fatty tissue. They are supported by suspensory ligaments called the ligaments of Ashley Cooper, which give them their line and lift. Breasts are at their fullest and perkiest at around age 22, the optimum age for reproduction in a woman's life when she is most likely to bring a foetus to full term. Gravity, lack of support and ageing are the

**Above:** Shiva dreamily contemplates his consort's beauty while caressing her breasts. They seem to arouse in him a special degree of tenderness.

Here is an exercise for the chest for warmth, generosity and openness. Position yourself with your arms at your sides, then clasp your hands in front of you with arms relaxed. Slowly raise your clasped hands up and lift them high over your head, then let them drop behind it down to the base of your neck. Press your hands together against your back. Bring them slowly back up and over to where you began. Repeat the exercise three times when you get up in the morning.

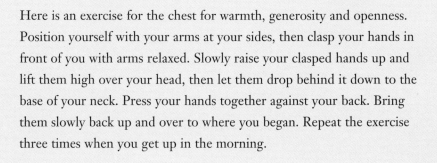

biggest enemy of firm breasts. Because they have no muscles, exercise does little to preserve shape and tone. Nevertheless, activities such as swimming and dancing strengthen the underlying pectoral muscles and give good posture and a sense of wellbeing. A massage from your lover using warm oil and gentle caressing strokes is both relaxing and stimulating. It can be a prelude to making love, or drifting off to sleep – or both!

## A note on size

As with other sexual organs, the size of the breasts doesn't matter. Big or small they function equally well as milk providers. But to a baby suckling at its mother's breast, the breast is enormous, physically and in terms of its importance. This helps to explain the visual appeal to some men of breasts that have been enlarged by plastic surgery to unnatural proportions. They may be pumped full of silicone and hard to the touch, but their sheer size triggers fantasies of comfort and bliss.

# The Belly

'Belly' is an unattractive word in the Western world, associated with greed and too much to drink. It is considered unfashionable to have a belly at all – both sexes aim at a stomach that is hard, muscular and completely flat. But in the East, the smoothly rounded belly of a woman is one of her most sensual attributes. The belly is the outward manifestation of the womb, and stands for fertility. It is symbolized in nature by caverns, gorges, springs and mines, hidden places deep in the earth that yield up sparkling treasures. Indian tradition holds that precious stones grow in rock like embryos in a womb. Inside the womb, Kundalini, the serpent of energy, lies slumbering coiled round a lingam of light.

**Above:** Two young women perform a joyful fertility dance. The shape made by their arms is echoed by the frame of the miniature, suggesting an egg or womb.

## The womb

The womb is the original safe place where the mystery of life begins. But it can devour as well as provide protection and nourishment. A mother can be a cruel tyrant who stunts her children's growth by keeping them enslaved to her despotic rule. In all mythologies, mother goddesses have two sides, one loving and compassionate, the other tyrannical and smotheringly jealous, and the goddess Kali with her evil black face and insatiable sexual appetites is no exception. In the west, we are fearful of accusing mothers of evil feelings – hence the invention of the wicked stepmother in fairy tales.

The womb of the Earth is the place to which we all return after death. Tomb and womb are linguistically related. Tumulus, meaning burial mound, comes from *tumere*, the Latin for to swell, which also means to be pregnant. The word tummy comes from the same root.

How should you hold your belly? If you tug it in, you distort the smooth functioning of the lungs and put stress on the shoulders and the back of the neck. If you let go completely, you sag and slump. The answer is to stand freely, feeling yourself centred in your belly. An awareness of the belly as the centre of the self gives confidence and solidity, a feeling of having both feet placed firmly on the ground.

## The belly roll

To exercise the belly and relax and sensitize the whole body, try the belly roll, one of the key movements of belly dancing. It imitates the contractions of labour and gives sexual confidence. Begin by placing both thumbs on your navel with your palms flat on your lower belly. Push the lower belly out, then pull it in and up as far as you can, pulling in your diaphragm too. Now push your diaphragm out and let your belly roll down and out. Begin slowly, then repeat the sequence, speeding up and maintaining a soothing rhythm. Some women like to practise the belly roll together in a group, to the rhythm of a drum. It can be a good starting point for meditation. A variation, the belly flutter, concentrates on the diaphragm. For this movement, you can either hold your breath, or keep your mouth open and pant. Contract the diaphragm and then push it out. Start with a slow repeat, then build up speed until your belly is vibrating fast.

## The hip roll

Another good exercise for the belly is the hip roll. Stand relaxed and upright, with your arms out to the side, palms facing up. Push the right hip out to the right side. Push the pelvis forward as far as you can and roll your hips over to the left. Push the pelvis back to the rear, sticking your bottom out. Straighten your knees, roll the hips to the right. Roll the hips in a large smooth circle, as if you were swinging a hula hoop round your waist.

# The Genitals

The tantric sages of ancient India worshipped the goddess Kali, because to them she symbolized the female sex organs, the fount of all life and the most sacred pleasure of living. Kali was also called Cunti and her sign was the yoni or vagina, which was represented by a mouth shape, such as a fish or a double-pointed oval, or by a simple triangle. The triangle was as important to the tantrists as the cross is to Christians, only of course the triangle symbolizes life and sex, whereas the cross means death.

## The yoni

The yoni is the symbol of a gateway to secret knowledge and the buried treasure of ecstasy. It is both mouth and well, taking and giving. The yoni swallows the lingam and brings forth life. Swallowing the lingam has its terrifying aspect, just as Kali is also a force of darkness and destruction. According to a Muslim proverb, three things on this Earth are insatiable: the desert, the grave and a woman's yoni. The idea of the castrating and all-devouring toothed vagina is present in all mythologies and reveals the deep male fear of losing himself in an ocean of love and desire, the birth trauma the wrong way round.

The mouth and vagina have many connections. The word mouth comes from the same root as mother. Yawn comes from yoni. The yoni has labiae – lips – and men have feared that, when bared, these lips might reveal teeth. Up until recently the male fear of castration led to the belief in many parts of the world that a male snake fertilizes the female by putting his head in her mouth and being swallowed alive. The ancients described sexual intercourse in similar terms. To them, the man did not take the woman, but was taken by her. When he ejaculated, the woman consumed his vital fluid. Semen means both seed and food, and consummating a sexual union was tantamount to eating the man. When the woman ate the food of the man, her stomach was seen to swell with pregnancy. For men, every orgasm is a little death, the death – albeit temporary – of the phallus.

## The lingam

Where goddess-worshippers adore the yoni, god-dominated religions worship the phallus. The Jews of the Old Testament worshipped their own genitals and swore oaths by laying a hand on each other's private parts. Words like testimony – and testament itself – derive from testicles, whose original meaning was witnesses. Phallic symbols everywhere are the marks of god-dominated religion. They can be seen in standing stones, columns and towers, and also in guns, missiles and other weapons. Terms like big shot, hit and score show how phallus worship can confuse sex and aggression.

Those who worship the yoni like it to be strong and muscular so that it can hug the lingam tightly, pulsating and squeezing it to build up a rhythm without moving any other parts of the body. Or the yoni can remain still while the lingam pulsates. Thus the couple can have exciting tantric sex while remaining outwardly motionless. For this kind of sex you need strong pelvic floor muscles. To strengthen them, practise regulating the flow of urine vigorously all the time, slowing it, then forcing it to flow more powerfully. Contract the pelvic floor muscles at least 70 times a day to make them really strong. You can do it at any time, as no one will know. Strengthening the perineum is particularly important after childbirth when these muscles have been severely strained. These exercises will also guard against incontinence in old age. As you contract your muscles, tune in to how much is contracting and where the muscles reach to. Do the exercise in bed with your partner and feel the contractions of each other's perineum with your fingers.

*Above:* In an unusually graphic depiction of oral sex, the woman is shown sucking her partner's lingam. This practice was not always approved of in ancient India, except when performed on men by male masseurs.

## The pelvic tilt

The pelvic tilt is a primitive dance step much used in belly dancing. Its message is explicit. Stand with knees flexed, feet comfortably close together, arms held out to the sides with palms upwards. Tighten the buttocks, thrust the pelvis forward and tilt upwards. Then relax the buttocks and push back. Practise until you can tilt your pelvis forward and backward smoothly and effortlessly.

# The Legs and Feet

Women walk differently from men, rolling their hips and taking smaller steps. This is because a woman's pelvic girdle is wider than a man's, allowing her to give birth between her legs. Down the ages, women have emphasized their feminine walk, by wearing sheathlike skirts that restrict their movement, and high heels, which make walking difficult and even dangerous. To balance in high heels, a woman has to tighten her calf muscles, giving the legs a more curvaceous shape. She also arches her back, which thrusts out her buttocks and breasts. In addition to curving the body into an S-shape, high heeled shoes make the wearer totter, creating an impression of vulnerability.

In China the fashion for female vulnerability centred on the foot was taken to grisly extremes. From the 11th century until it was banned in 1902, the Chinese upper classes practised the cruel custom of footbinding. From the age of five, a girl's feet were tightly bound in strips of cloth until by the time she had finished growing, they were completely deformed, the foot curled under like a closed fist with only the big toe protruding. This 'lotus foot' proclaimed a woman's status, because it prevented her from working, and even from walking without the aid of servants. The ultimate sexual pleasure for Chinese men was to have intercourse with the sole of the lotus foot, and crippled women were taught how to satisfy their husbands in this way.

*Above:* Here Shiva is shown performing an act of unusual tenderness: anointing the feet of his beloved with scented oil. Her attendants stand by to complete her toilette.

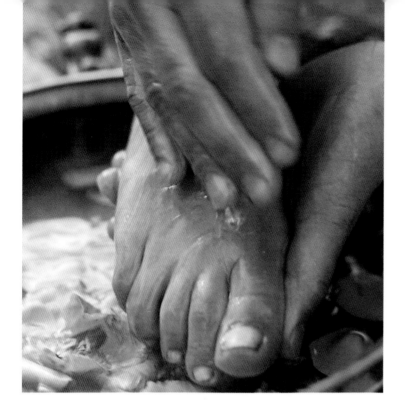

*Left:* A foot massage can bring relief and revitalization to the whole body. Use warm oil and knead each toe and joint gently but thoroughly.

## Footcare

The foot was also an erotic part of the body in India. Many miniatures feature an Indian prince enjoying sex with several companions, using his big toes to stimulate the clitorises of two of his consorts. Women in India paint delicate henna patterns on their feet, wear bright tinkling anklets and colour their toenails with henna too. Care of the feet is important for general wellbeing. Think of sexuality as freedom and choose shoes that allow your feet to express your vitality instead of cramping their style. Pamper your feet – and your partner's – with a warm foot bath followed by a massage, a treatment that will revive your body and spirits. Washing the feet is an act of forgiveness and acceptance because it symbolizes purification from walking the wrong paths of life. Rub your heels with a pumice stone to get rid of hard dead skin and make them soft and supple. Feel your connection to the earth by walking and dancing barefoot on the grass. Try walking not by putting your heel down first in the normal way, which is hard and jarring, but landing on your toes and the ball of the foot. This silent, sensual walk gives greater exercise to the calf muscles.

As for your legs, forgive them their imperfections. Beauty lies more in the way you move than in shapeliness. Good exercises to tone the leg muscles are swimming, cycling and dancing.

# The Kama Sutra

# Yoga Practice

Yoga is the world's most ancient system of personal development. The word 'yoga' means joining – the joining of the body and the consciousness to an unchanging reality that lies beyond. Yoga allows you to float free of personal worries and leave the clutter of everyday life behind. It strengthens and tones the body, improving the functioning of muscles and joints. The spine grows more flexible and the exercises also work on the internal organs, the glands and the nerves. The physical and emotional effects of yoga open your mind and body to deeper sexual feelings.

**Right:** Introducing simple yoga poses can add a new dimension to making love. Yoga brings a sense of wholeness and personal balance to an intimate relationship.

Yoga can help with sex because it's difficult to get in tune with your partner if one of you is distracted or tense. You both need to be centred – in touch with yourselves – before you can connect with each other. Yoga can help you relax. It is possible to be tense all the time without realizing it, even to lie rigidly in bed, grimly awaiting sleep with your mind and body galvanized for the sound of the alarm clock and the next headlong dash into action. Try tensing and relaxing your muscles to see just how keyed up you are.

Physical relaxation brings a feeling of wellbeing, as well as freedom from aches and pains, but yoga gives more than this. As you continue to practise it, yoga brings a sense of the harmony and peace of mind that are the foundations of true self-knowledge. It provides a touchstone of relaxation and stillness that will always enable you to get your bearings in the confusion of everyday life.

The exercise of yoga consists of getting into and out of a series of postures, or asanas. The movements are slow and graceful, never jerky. They extend your reach gradually and should not be forced. After a yoga session, you should feel relaxed and full of energy, not exhausted or strained. Deep, measured breathing is especially important to help you move correctly.

When you start following the sequences in this book, you may find some of the positions difficult to get into, unless you are already practising yoga. Don't push yourselves to do anything that is uncomfortable, or hurts. Just imagine forming the shapes in the photographs even if you can't actually achieve them. With practice, you will become more supple. Alternatively, use the positions shown here as an inspiration for your own individual sequence of movements.

*Above:* Sometimes life is so full of stresses that it's difficult to relax together. Meditation and yoga can clear the mind and make space for peace and intimacy.

# The Frog

The pleasure here lies in the man keeping up a gentle rocking motion while the woman stays perfectly still, moving only the muscles of her yoni to let her partner in gradually. After a tantalizingly slow build-up, he can pump vigorously to a climax. The man needs to develop strong thigh muscles to maintain this position of deep penetration without tiring. Comfort is important, so if the strain tells, the man can roll backwards into the sitting position and let the woman bounce in his lap.

1 First arrange your cushions. When the woman lies back, her body will need to be slightly raised and a pillow under her buttocks will allow her partner deeper entry. The man squats with legs apart. The woman sits on his lap, with her legs over his. In this position the lovers can kiss and stimulate each other's genitals with their hands, using a massage oil to enhance the sensation. In this way, the man can bring his partner to orgasm.

# Love and money

A courtesan should always keep her emotions in check, remembering that her independence is her livelihood. If she does happen to fall in love, she shouldn't let it get the better of her. On the other hand, the courtesan should always act as though she is in love with her man, even when she despises him, because this is the way to gain his confidence. He will tell her what is in his heart and look after her well, so that she doesn't need to trick him out of his money. However, if he is not generous, Vatsyayana advises that there are 27 ways in which a clever woman can persuade a man to part with cash and jewels. Among his list of suggestions are these. The woman can rush to her lover, weeping and gnashing her teeth, wailing that her house has been burned down by the carelessness of her servants, and that she has no money to rebuild it. Or she may appear at his door in tears, pretending that she has been robbed of her possessions by the king's guards and desperately needs to replace them. In a more thoughtful moment, perhaps while he is still lying in her bed, she can mention in passing that she needs to buy food, drink, flowers, perfume and cloth, none of which she can afford. Or she might reveal that she can't go visiting to friends' houses, because when her friends come to her, they bring costly presents, and she has nothing to give them. Behaving listlessly, she can admit after anxious questioning that she is ill, but has not the wherewithal for medical treatment. Finally, she can always fall back on making her lover jealous, by telling him how generous his rivals are.

2 When the time is right, the woman slides her partner's lingam inside her yoni. She will be extra sensitive to the delicious sensation. Clenching and releasing the muscles of her yoni, she begins to rock gently, supporting herself with her arms around her lover's shoulders.

**3** The man lowers his partner on to the pillows, sliding his hands down to support the small of her back. In this position he can raise her pelvis towards him and thrust gently, bouncing on his haunches.

# The dark side of Kali

Kali, the mother goddess, the Earth goddess, ruled over every aspect of life, but she was also feared as goddess of destruction, disease and death. In some paintings she appears suffused with blood and passion, with a red face and eyes, long pointed teeth bared in a terrible snarl, and a noose in her hand. At other times she is seen devouring the entrails of her dead consort Shiva, while squatting on him in sexual ecstasy. Kali is also shown triumphantly garlanded with human skulls, or holding a sword and a severed head, and wearing corpses as earrings or amputated hands linked round her waist in a belt. As goddess of death she appears emaciated, with sunken eyes, shrivelled breasts and ragged hair, but always ecstatic, her volcanic emotions sweeping all before her.

For the tantric sages, it was important to accept the whole range of human experience, and to embrace Kali as the one who gave life in the beginning and who would finally take it away at the end. Kali was the ocean of blood that existed before birth, and she is the nothing-at-all that happens after death — both womb and tomb.

***Above:*** Though the man is on top, the woman can still change the mood and the tone of the experience by opening her yoni wider or tilting herself towards or away from him.

Sex and death are powerfully linked in our unconscious minds. The one transcending power, sexual passion is where we lose ourselves in the rush of orgasm, called by the French 'the little death'. Giving oneself completely in sex does have a frightening aspect, because it means negating the self, letting go of control, and existing purely in the present moment, in sensation and emotion. Giving oneself in love can be terrifying, because it leaves us vulnerable to overwhelming loss and destruction. Accustomize yourself gradually to the dark face of Kali as your intimacy grows and your risks will be rewarded with deeper, richer feelings.

# The Hunter

Hunting was one of the favourite pursuits of upper-class Indians. Some liked to combine it with sex. In this position (see page 41) the Indian prince takes up his rifle to shoot a gazelle. Modern-day Western lovers rock gently backwards and forwards. This position is more exciting if all the movement is left to the woman.

1 The lovers stand facing each other. The man drops to his right knee and keeps his left knee up with his foot firmly on the floor at right angles to it. The woman lifts her right leg up and places her right foot delicately on his left hip bone. Her toes point outwards and her heel points to his groin. Her standing leg remains straight.

2 She lowers herself on to his thigh, circling his right shoulder with her left arm. He embraces her, drawing her to him, and they kiss.

# Krishna and the gopis

**K**rishna is the god Shiva in another incarnation. Many details of his story were borrowed for the life of Jesus. When the Lord Krishna was born to a goddess, his advent was proclaimed by angels and a new star appeared in the sky to mark his birthplace. Shepherds and wise men came from afar to worship the baby and bring gifts. Shortly afterwards Krishna survived a massacre of the innocents. He performed many miracles, including parting the waves of a stormy river while still a baby by touching the waters with his tiny foot. Eventually he was hailed as a redeemer of sins and met with a sacrificial death, in which his blood rained down on the Earth and made it fruitful.

But unlike Christ, Krishna was an erotic god, adored for his youthfulness and beauty. As a child, he was known for mischief verging on juveline delinquency. He untied village cattle and pulled their tails, was rude his elders, urinated in the houses of his neighbours and stole their sweets and butter. A precocious and highly sexed adolescent, he played his flute (flute being another word for the sacred lingam or penis) to charm the gopis, beautiful girls who looked after the cows. A Hindu poet wrote: 'How can I describe his relentless flute, which pulls virtuous women from their homes and drags them by their hair to Krishna as thirst and hunger pull the doe to the snare?'

One day while the gopis were bathing in a river, Krishna hid in a tree to watch them and stole their saris. At the sound of his flute they left the water and began to dance, shyly at first, but soon with wild abandon. Krishna's music was so ravishing that each believed herself to be dancing with him alone. He made love with them all, but his favourite was Radha. This dark, isatiable beauty was honoured with the name 'cow elephant', as the female elephant was considered the epitome of sexual appetite and desire.

**3** He grips her more tightly around the waist and draws her closely towards him. She puts her right hand on his left knee and her left hand behind his neck to support her balance and pulls herself closer to him. In this position he enters her.

**4** She drops down to her left knee and curves her right leg around his waist so their bodies are close, yet balanced away from each other. She points her toes and takes hold of her left foot with her left hand. He draws her body even closer as they gaze directly into each other's eyes.

**Above:** Perhaps the ultimate exercise in warding off premature ejaculation was to transfer the release to a firearm! The modern-day equivalent might be sex while watching football on television – something few women would appreciate.

# The lotus

Probably best known in the West as the meditation pose of the yogis, the lotus flower with its many layers of petals symbolizes the yoni and is central to tantrism. All life springs from the lotus — even the god Brahma, who claimed to be the creator, was born from the yoni of the primal goddess. All power also springs from the lotus, and the only way a man can have power and recharge his vital energy is to unite himself with the yoni of the goddess in sacred sex.

The tantric sages held that carnal knowledge was the gateway to spiritual knowledge, so only through union with the lotus could the inner mysteries of life be revealed. The phrase 'Jewel in the Lotus' means the lingam in the yoni, the foetus in the womb, the corpse in the earth and the god in the goddess. The phrase 'Lotus-Eater' refers to ritual cunnilingus, which was another way of communing with the goddess. Mystics sitting in the lotus pose aimed through their sexual knowledge to awaken the slumbering serpent Kundalini, which lies dormant, coiled round the lower chakras of the spine, and cause it to rise right up through the body, flowering in an invisible emanation of light as a fully formed lotus from the top of the head. Well aware of the sexual connotations of sitting cross-legged, the medieval Church in Europe denounced the pose, accusing all who sat this way of sorcery.

# The Cow

This sequence offers an exciting way into a simple position. The man can thrust vigorously and the woman can respond by slamming her buttocks into him. Or she can begin to subside on to a cushion, leading him into a more gentle lying down position, often referred to in the West as spoons.

**1** The man kneels on the floor with his knees close together and his buttocks on his heels, his feet flat down behind him. The woman half kneels down close to him on his left side. Their bodies are touching and their arms caressing one another. She has her right arm round his right shoulder and her left hand on his right forearm. He has his left arm around her back and his right hand on her waist.

**2** She lunges her right leg over his thighs, creating a right angle to the floor, making sure that her lunge is deep enough so that her knee does not extend over her foot. She balances on her left knee and her left hand moves to his leg. He supports her right thigh with his right hand.

# The courtesan's mother

A courtesan had to earn good money for the upkeep of her house and garden and to pay her retinue of servants, jugglers and masseurs. And only by living in style and dressing richly could she attract the right kind of wealthy and cultivated lovers. On top of this financial chicken-and-egg situation, the courtesan had a difficult emotional juggling act to perform. She was a woman of independent character and mind, too individual and spirited to be a wife, yet in order to live she had to please her lover in every way, making herself totally subservient to his whim. How could she both control the course of the affair and agree to every demand her lover made? The answer is, with the help of her mother.

The courtesan's mother – or, if she was unavailable, her old nurse – was a shadowy figure kept in the background of her life. When talking to her lover, the courtesan would complain that her mother was a harsh old woman whose only interest was money. She would confide haltingly that her mother disapproved of their union, and of her lover's treatment of her. So he knew there was an enemy in the camp who could threaten his happiness, and it made him anxious. If the tactics of love demanded that the courtesan withdrew from her lover to increase his ardour, she could blame her absence on her cross old mother. Or if she was short of money, she could ask for it on behalf of the difficult old crone who pestered her night and day for cash. In effect, Vatsyayana recommended that the courtesan split her personality in two, and piled all the difficult aspects of it on to her mother. Of course, in reality, mother and daughter were totally in tune, working as a team.

3 From this position she slides her right leg in a perfectly straight line and extends her left leg behind her until her weight is fully on his body. She points both her feet and balances between her right heel and her left knee. She gently lifts her spine up towards her partner so her back is leaning on his chest and she can twist towards him to gaze lovingly into his eyes.

4 As he enters her, she turns her back to him and bending forwards, rests both hands on the ground. She swings both legs back next to his.

5 He clasps her around the waist with both hands, and rising on to his knees, lifts her up and forward until her feet come together in front of his knees. Resting her head on a cushion, she clasps her hands as if in prayer under her cheek.

**Above:** The carefully arranged accessories and impassive expressions speak of art rather than passion. In the background a servant does a little light dusting.

# The nails

The Kama Sutra instructs lovers on how to 'press with the nails'. Vatsyayana constructed an elaborate language of erotic scratching, which left marks that could be flaunted as sexual trophies alongside love bites. For this purpose, lovers were advised to keep their nails clean and glossy and to stain them tawny with henna. Appropriate times to mark a lover included during leave-taking before a journey, after returning home, on becoming reconciled after a quarrel, and whenever a woman became intoxicated. Nails could be pressed into the lover's armpits, throat, breasts, lips, midriff, buttocks and thighs. The marks left behind formed certain shapes or patterns. They looked like half moons, the jump of a hare or the leaf of a blue lotus. Sometimes they appeared to have been made by a peacock's foot or a tiger's claw. Such marks were worn with pride by young women, for the sight of a woman wandering through a scented pleasure garden with marks of passion on her bare breasts would inflame the heart of any man. Men were warned, however, not to mark married women in this way. Married women could only bear secret marks on their private parts, which they could contemplate while sighing with longing for the absent lover. How their husbands failed to notice these marks is not made clear.

# Chariot

For this highly erotic pose, make sure the woman sits on a cushion to bring her up to a comfortable height, and that she also has plenty of soft pillows to lean on. Chariot is a delicate balancing act that needs strong leg muscles to prevent the couple tiring and a sense of strain taking over from the ecstasy of contact through just the hands and genitals. The lovers gaze into each other's eyes to deepen the sensation of blissful intimacy.

2 Now the woman leans back, supporting her weight by gripping his forearms. She slides her hands down his arms, then rests her palms on the ground behind her.

1 The man squats with his knees turned outwards. His back is straight. His partner sits on a cushion in between his legs, with her legs over his and her knees clasping his waist. Her feet are soles-together behind his back. She puts her arms round his back and he holds her tenderly by the waist.

# The harem

The women of the harem have to share one man. Even a generous man who uses aphrodisiacs that enable him to enjoy several women in one night cannot possibly satisfy all his wives, so they have to find other ways of having fun. Some dress up as men and use a bulbous root as a dildo. Others work themselves into a frenzy on the phallus of a statue. Sometimes the women enjoy oral sex with the eunuchs who guard them, or with each other. But the best and most dangerous sexual treat is to smuggle a man into the royal apartments. He may be disguised as a woman or arrive rolled in a carpet. If the intruder is discovered, his adventure will surely cost him his life, so he is well advised to make friends with the harem guards and nurses and get them on his side. A good time to be smuggled into the palace is during the confused comings and goings that surround a drinking festival or a fair or the preparations for a pilgrimage. Even so, the would-be lover is advised to make himself invisible with a magic potion. He should burn the eyes of a serpent and smear a paste of the ashes on his eyelids, then he can go about unseen.

3 The woman lifts first her right leg, then her left, over her partner's shoulders. The man stretches his arms out behind him with palms flat on the floor and mirrors the woman's movement, putting his feet on her shoulders. This is the moment of entry.

4   The couple now clasp forearms under the man's knees, as he lowers his feet to the floor.

5   The woman leans back and lowers her feet to the floor over the man's hips and under his arms. They rock gently in a see-saw motion.

# Magic potions

**Above:** The endless variety and richness of repeat patterns on fabrics, wall hangings and carpets says much about the Eastern way of life. The seamlessness of Indian art and music is found again in India's attitude to love: the emphasis is on the continuum, not on beginnings and endings.

The men and women of ancient India had access to a wide variety of potions, charms and philtres to help them in their amorous adventures. If a couple's genitals were ill-matched in size, the man could enlarge his lingam by rubbing it with the bristles of certain insects that live in trees, then for ten nights rub it with oil, followed by another treatment with the bristly insects. After this, his lingam was so swollen that he had to lie down and let it hang through a hole in the bed, then massage it with cooling ointments. The pain would disappear but the swelling would remain. A woman could rub ointment into her yoni to make it smaller, and another salve promised to enlarge the breasts.

Vatsyayana recommends several ways of transforming an ugly person into a magnetic beauty, including eating the pollen of the blue lotus with ghee and honey and tying a gilded peacock or hyena bone to the right hand. To prevent a woman being given in marriage to anyone else, a man should sprinkle her with monkey dung. To increase sexual vigour, a man should drink sugared milk in which he has boiled up a goat's testicle. Other magic recipes guaranteed to bring a woman quickly to orgasm, and to delay ejaculation in a man. Herbs were widely used to regulate menstrual periods and to encourage or prevent conception.

# Canopy of Stars

On a hot summer night, experience the cosmic bliss of tantra under the stars. Walk out with your lover to a secret moonlit place. Spread a thick rug on the ground and lay a pillow at either end. Feel the earth move within you as comets explode, trailing fiery showers above.

1 The man sits down on the rug, stretching his legs out in front of him and keeping his back firm and straight. The woman sits sideways between his legs with her legs and feet together along his right hip. They embrace, she around his shoulders and he around her hips.

2 Leaning back, the woman supports herself with her right hand on the rug. She curls her right leg tightly round her lover's waist. Then, slowly and gracefully, she lifts her left foot in her left hand like a dancer, straightening her leg and pointing her foot over his left shoulder. He leans back to allow her leg to pass in front of his face, then supports her body under the small of her back. The pose is open and provocative, the moment is mystical.

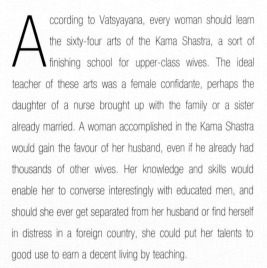

# The Kama Shastra

According to Vatsyayana, every woman should learn the sixty-four arts of the Kama Shastra, a sort of finishing school for upper-class wives. The ideal teacher of these arts was a female confidante, perhaps the daughter of a nurse brought up with the family or a sister already married. A woman accomplished in the Kama Shastra would gain the favour of her husband, even if he already had thousands of other wives. Her knowledge and skills would enable her to converse interestingly with educated men, and should she ever get separated from her husband or find herself in distress in a foreign country, she could put her talents to good use to earn a decent living by teaching.

Among the arts a woman would learn were singing, dancing and drawing, cooking, perfumery, jewellery, tattooing, reading, composing poems, play-acting, clay modelling, archery, languages and hairdressing. She would also discover how to fix stained glass into a floor, make lemonades and sherbets, fashion parrots out of thread, play a tune on glasses filled with water, fight with a sword, gamble, trick people out of their rightful property by magic and sorcery, and teach parrots and starlings to speak. Add to this an understanding of fighting with cocks, quails and rams, knowledge of mineralogy and warfare and expertise in gymnastics, and the picture of a leisured life in ancient India is complete.

Of course the Kama Shastra is just part of the Kama Sutra, which even young girls studied avidly before marriage.

3 When the moment is right, coitus can begin. The woman lets go of her foot, signalling her readiness, so her left leg lies hard against his shoulder. Her hands are on the ground behind her to support her weight. He clasps her back and draws her on to him. United, the lovers maintain this deeply penetrative pose with very little movement until they feel full of each other's presence.

4 Then the man clasps her wrists, she clasps his, and they both lower themselves gently down into the pillows. Her legs slide along his sides, mirroring the pose of his legs. They each raise one arm above their heads in a gesture of openness to the heavens, still clasping each other with the other hand.

# The child bride

It was common in ancient India for girls to be married off by arrangement at a young age, but a child-bride still had to be won over by her prospective husband. He could start to interest her by playing games like hide-and-seek or blind man's buff, or finding a trinket hidden in one of several little heaps of wheat. He could bring her wooden dolls, balls of coloured thread, cages of partridges, little clay figures, buffalo horn carvings, paints and dyes, even 'machines for throwing water about' – the more unusual the gift, the greater his chance of success. He could perform juggling tricks to make her laugh, act out fictitious stories about members of her family, pick flowers and show her how to make garlands, teach her how to play with dice and cards and buy her earrings and a guitar. Having made an impression, he should use her nurse's daughter as a go-between, telling the child of his great skill in the art of sexual enjoyment.

Once this subject has been broached, it is the turn of the young girl to show how she feels. If she finds him attractive, she will blush and look away when he speaks to her, or gaze at him secretly from under her eyelashes. She will hang her head when he asks a question and answer indistinctly, letting her words trail shyly away. She can shower kisses on the young children in her care, behave affectionately to his servants and wilfully with her own. Finally, she can send him a ring or a garland by a female friend, upon which he must do everything he can to gain her hand in marriage.

**Above:** In this love pose, gazing into each other's eyes is followed by gazing into heaven to discover the direct experience of ever-lasting power and transcendence. The stars are symbols of the spirit, guiding lights shining in the darkness.

# Feeding the Peacock

The title of this love pose comes from the Indian miniature shown on p.57, in which the woman holds out a golden cup for the male peacock to peck out of, while her lover's lingam is inside her. The peacock's beak is a metaphor for the lingam, and the gold cup stands for the yoni. Lovers have to be the right height to achieve the pose illustrated in the miniature, but if they are not, the woman can stand on a bench or on the bottom step of a flight of stairs. This pose is one that can be adopted in a hurry, for example, while out for a country walk, in which case a tree would provide useful support.

1 A good way to get into the simple standing pose is for the woman to sit with her legs apart on a piece of furniture, such as the back of a sofa, so that she is slightly higher than her partner's genitals. The man squats on his haunches between his partner's legs, from where he can kiss her breasts. She can bend to kiss his mouth.

# The virtuous wife

A virtuous wife in ancient India was one who regarded her husband as a god and did everything to please him. Under his direction, she was to take care of the family, keep the house neat and clean and full of flowers, tend the garden and the sanctuary of the household gods, and get everything ready for the sacrifices held in the morning, noon and evening. The garden she should plant with green vegetables, radishes, potatoes, beets, mangoes, cucumbers, aubergines, pumpkins, garlic, onions, sugar cane, fig trees, mustard, parsley, fennel and scented flowers and grasses. In secret corners of the garden she should have seats and arbours, and in the centre a soothing water feature, such as a pool or well.

2 When the time is right, the man stands and lifts his partner on to his lingam. She holds on firmly round his neck and shoulder and grasps his waist with her thighs. In this position the couple can have vigorous intercourse. The woman moves strongly against her partner, while he supports her bottom with his arms, helping to thrust her against him.

A good cook who pays attention to her husband's preferences and nutritious requirements, the wife leaps up when she hears her husband returning home and washes his feet. She avoids making unsuitable friends, such as beggars, fortune tellers and witches, takes care not to discuss her husband's affairs behind his back and keeps scrupulous household accounts. She turns leftover milk into ghee and makes rope and cords from the bark of trees. She supervises the tilling of the fields, the pounding of the rice and the care of the livestock – rams, cocks, quails, parrots, starlings, cuckoos, peacocks, monkeys and deer. She gives her worn-out clothes to the servants, and presents her husband's visitors with flowers, ointment, incense and betel leaves. For everyday she dresses modestly with few adornments, but for her husband she will wear her most colourful clothes, jewellery, flowers and perfumes. When her husband is away, she spends her time fasting and waiting anxiously for news of him.

3 In this position it is easy to tire. The man can lower his partner gently to the ground, or to a stool or cushion of the right height, so they can stand, still united, 'feeding the peacock'. Stillness is an important part of tantric sex. It allows exquisite sensations to build up in all the sexual nerve endings, until some kind of movement is urgently required. Now the couple can move very gently, tuning completely into the feelings in their genitals. Finally, when they can stand gentleness no more, the man picks up his partner again and carries her to the couch, where vigorous thrusting is resumed.

***Above:*** Here it is the woman who engages in a diversionary tactic to take her partner's mind off the urgency of sex and make him last longer. If you don't have a peacock to hand, feed your lover grapes. Peel them first of course.

# The lovers' tiff

The lovers of the Kama Sutra live in a world of formalized behaviour where problems must be driven underground. Women must learn to bite their lips and be submissive. If a husband behaves badly, his wife should not blame him excessively, even though she might be hurt. She should avoid black looks, talking behind his back, and standing around in doorways where people can see and admire her. Above all, she should not take her revenge by wandering in pleasure groves, where there is certain danger of meeting attractive men with time on their hands. Instead, she should remain dutifully indoors, keeping her body, her teeth, her hair and everything belonging to her tidy, sweet and clean.

Should a love quarrel erupt despite the woman's best efforts to grit her perfectly clean teeth and avoid marring her beauty with murderous looks, it must follow a prescribed pattern. The wife is allowed to pull her husband's hair and kick him, but she should withdraw no further than the doorway. Aggressive feelings are to be contained in ritual striking, crying out, biting and piercing with the nails. It is not surprising, since there is no other outlet for negative feelings, that Vatsyayana considers sadism part of normal lovemaking. He gives lists prescribing with what force and on which parts of the body cruel practices may be carried out.

# The Plough

If you are going to try this position on the bed, make sure that it is firm – a soft surface might wobble and upset the lovers' balance. A thick duvet is more comfortable for the man's knees than a bristly carpet. Allow plenty of soft cushions for the woman to rest on. This gentle pose can subside into 'spoons', in which the man rolls over to lie behind his partner, so that both are on their sides, with her fitting into his lap. 'Spoons' is a late-night position, a comforting one in which to fall asleep with the promise of continuing lovemaking in the morning.

2 The woman bends forward, placing her palms flat on the ground at either side of her knees. Her forehead touches the ground in front of them. When the moment is right, he enters her.

1 The man kneels down and the woman sits astride his lap, facing away from him. He has his arms around her waist. In this position he can caress her breasts.

# Biting

Not just nibbling but passionate devouring with lips, teeth and tongue and even angry vicious biting were apparently commonplace in the lovers' repertoire of ancient India. Perhaps boredom led the indolent upper classes into sadistic practices. Vatsyayana favoured bright strong teeth that would take well to dyeing red or black. He liked to see them even, unbroken and above all sharp. Good teeth could be used to inflict various bites on the lover's skin, such as the hidden bite, the swollen bite, the line of jewels, the broken cloud and the bite of the boar. The left cheek was considered a prime site for biting, as well as the throat, the armpit and the joints of the thighs.

Vatsyayana had a curious idea that if men and women enjoyed biting each other, even the passing of a hundred years would not dim the fire of their love. He was keen that anger should be expressed as violently as possible and advocated the dangerous practice of biting in a love quarrel. 'When a man bites a woman forcibly, she should angrily do the same to him with double force.' The quarrel, he believed, would turn into ecstatic lovemaking: '...she should take hold of her lover by the hair, and bend his head down, and kiss his lower lip, and then, being intoxicated with love, she should shut her eyes and bite him in various places.'

3 She stretches her right leg back along the side of his right leg, supporting herself on the ground while keeping her left leg bent. She lowers herself on to the cushions, resting her head on her right arm.

When the lovers next met, she would show him the wounds he had inflicted on her, her eyes flashing with rage, and the painful business would begin all over again.

4 Stretching his arms along her back, the man can now rock gently into her. All she has to do is concentrate on the sensations in her yoni, hugging his lingam tightly.

# A day of pleasure

On rising, the student of the Kama Sutra performed an elaborate toilet, which included shaving all body hair, bathing, perfuming his body and making up his eyes and mouth in front of a mirror. He would chew betel leaves to freshen his breath, perhaps stain his teeth red or black, then take breakfast, after which he spent some time training his parrots to speak and his quails, cocks and rams to fight. The remaining hour or two before lunch were devoted to literature and drama. A nap followed during the heat of the day. Then the citizen dressed in his finery and ornaments and went out visiting. Sitting with friends, he would talk and drink cordials made from the bark of trees as well as from fruits and flowers. Other social diversions included picnics, singing, walks in the garden and pelting one another with the scented blossoms of the kadamba tree. Sometimes there were swimming parties, though the servants were instructed to make sure no dangerous animals lurked in the water. At other times the friends were entertained by acrobats or jesters. All this was a gentle build-up to the pleasures of the night. When dusk fell, the men waited in a room full of perfume and flowers for the women of their choice to arrive.

**Above:** Though the woman's body remains still, she can exercise control by clenching the muscles of her yoni. In tantric sex, it is these small internal movements that make all the difference, creating a rich symphony of subtle sensations.

# Temple

The temple is not as difficult as it looks for those with yoga training who have very supple legs. The final tantric pose is outwardly motionless, but the feelings are intense if the couple have strong pelvic muscle control. Lovers who are daunted by the exotic leg bends could follow the instructions to stage three for a gentle rocking pose that is easy to achieve.

1 The surface should be firm – a futon would be excellent, but most beds are too soft for this pose, as any movement would tip the couple over. The man sits on the floor with a straight back, his knees pointing outwards and the soles of his feet together. The woman sits inside his legs, with her legs round his waist and her soles together behind him. He holds her gently round the waist, while she grips his back. In this position the lovers can kiss until they are well aroused.

2 When the time is right the man lifts his partner up and forward and penetrates her. She now leans back to support herself with her palms flat on the ground behind her. She lifts her buttocks off the floor and her right leg over his shoulder. She follows with her left leg so that both legs are parallel. The lovers gaze into each other's eyes and the man rocks his partner gently backwards and forwards.

## Sex aids

Dildoes were common sex aids in ancient India. They were often fashioned in the form of a sheath to be worn over the lingam and increase its size. They were made of precious materials, such as gold, silver and ivory, and sometimes of wood, tin or lead. The consequences of rubbing the delicate mucous membranes of the vagina with poisonous lead do not bear thinking about. For solitary pleasure or mutual use in the harem, women used bulbous gourds or roots, well oiled, or bundles of reeds tied together and softened with the extracts of plants.

In southern India there was a strong fashion for piercing. In fact it was believed that women could not get true sexual pleasure unless their partner had a ring or other ornament attached to his lingam. Vatsyayana instructs his student to pierce the lingam with a sharp instrument, then stand in water until the blood stops flowing. That night he should have vigorous sex, 'in order to clean the hole'. Thereafter, he should clean the hole regularly with liquorice and honey and gradually increase the size of the hole by putting into it small pieces of cane and fruit stalks, until it is big enough to take a heron bone or other ornament.

3 Now the man leans back to support his own weight on the floor with palms flat and fingers pointing backwards. He lifts first his right leg and then his left on to her shoulders. In this position the couple can rock gently against one another.

4 The man moves his right leg to the ground and the woman clasps his foot in her right hand. She now drops her left leg to the floor alongside his body. The man holds up his right arm, she raises her left arm and they clasp hands above their heads (above). If this pose is uncomfortable, the couple can drop both legs to the ground and lean close to kiss (left).

# Courtesans

The world's first prostitutes were priestesses who performed sacred sexual rites in temples dedicated to the goddess. By the time of Vatsyayana, prostitution had moved out of the temple and into the boudoir, but the tantric sages still saw sex as a mystic and healing experience and courtesans were held in the highest regard.

The life of a courtesan was in many ways preferable to the life of a wife. Courtesans were usually women of considerable intellect and much better educated than their married sisters. Witty, amusing, talented and amorous, they were the equals of the interesting and powerful men they attracted. Part of their allure was that they were also the only women of their day to enjoy financial and social independence.

Though courtesans were in the business of love to earn money, they didn't sit back and wait for customers to come to them. Instead, a clever courtesan sought out a rich and influential man and set about seducing him, by giving him garlands of flowers and precious ointments, telling him entertaining stories, sending a jester or masseur to his house, or inviting him to a cock fight. Once the man was snared, she kept his interest by treating him like a god and making herself indispensable while remaining aloof from him in her heart. This made him shower her with riches, always wanting more.

**Above:** The four-poster bed with its rich canopy and pure white quilt provides the perfect setting for a pose dedicated to the goddess. Indian lovers surround themselves with a variety of plump cushions for comfort and support.

# Shoal of Fish

This position is so-named because the woman looks as though she is swimming. She supports her torso on a convenient piece of furniture, such as the back of a couch, and the man moves, first gently and then more vigorously, between her legs.

1 The man puts his left knee on the floor and his right foot on the floor with his right knee at a right angle. The woman sits on his lap facing away from him with her right knee forward and her left knee pointing down to the ground. The man supports her round the waist and she rests her hands on his. In this position he can kiss the nape of her neck and caress her breasts.

# The ideal mistress

The courtesan of the Kama Sutra is a skilled manipulator of male vanity. Socially and intellectually the equal of her lover, her job is nevertheless to make herself into his slave. This she does by presenting a perfect mirror to his feelings, laughing when he is happy, pining away when he is sick, looking downcast even when he sighs or yawns, hating his enemies, never showing irritation or anger, pretending jealousy of other women, wishing to have a child by him, eating the food he leaves on his plate, pleasuring him in any way he wants and expressing amazement at his accomplishments and his rare knowledge of the sexual arts. If anyone should try to come between them, she should threaten to take her own life by poisoning, stabbing or hanging herself.

For these services, the courtesan is deservedly well rewarded. Yet still she may feel like tricking more money and gifts out of her lover, probably out of a mischievous desire to exploit him in revenge for subjugating her personality to his every whim. Vatsyayana lists twenty-seven ways in which a mistress can wheedle money out of a gullible lover, including pretending that her house has burned down and her jewels have been stolen, or that she needs to buy new clothes or upgrade her cooking utensils in line with those of her friends.

2 He holds her by the waist and she drops her torso gracefully forwards, supporting her weight on her arms on a piece of furniture.

3 The man stands up, sliding his hands along his partner's sides to grip her by the thighs and lift her on to his erect lingam. She keeps her legs straight behind her to allow him freedom of movement. The man controls the pace, thrusting first gently and then passionately as both lovers thrill to the depth of penetration this position affords.

**Above:** The lovers choose the paved terrace of a roof garden in the palace for this pose. There is a special freedom in making love outside.

# Adultery

A dultery was a popular pastime in ancient India and daily life offered plenty of opportunities for adventure. The man who delivered corn and filled the householder's granary was invited indoors by his wife, as were the handyman, the cleaner, the labourer in the fields and the door-to-door salesmen of cotton, wool, flax, hemp and thread. While the cowherds enjoyed the cow girls, the superintendents of widows enjoyed the widows in their charge and the superintendents of markets found secret corners in which to entertain their female customers. On warm evenings villagers roamed the streets looking for excitement, while those left at home bedded the wives of their sons.

A king with a harem needed to make more elaborate plans for seduction. During the spring festival of the eighth moon it was the custom for the townswomen to visit the ladies of the harem and chat, drink cordials and play games until dawn. If one of these visitors pleased the king, he would instruct one of his wives to accost the woman as she left the palace and invite her to look around. She would be shown the bower of the coral creeper and the bower covered in vines, the garden house with its floor inlaid with precious stones, the pavilion on the lake, the secret passages in the walls of the palace, the priceless works of art, the aviaries of birds and the cages of lions and tigers. While the visitor was being impressed by the king's wealth and taste, his wife would tell her of her husband's love for her and promise her good fortune if she agreed to a rendezvous, at the same time giving her a promise of absolute secrecy. In the unlikely event of her declining to lie with the king, she would be sent away with friendly wishes and gifts.

# The Wheel

Yoga practice will give the woman the strength, flexibility of spine and stamina she needs for this love pose. The angle of penetration ensures that her G-spot is stimulated, which gives some women heightened pleasure. However practised and supple his partner is, the man should be gentle in this pose, taking care to support the small of her back and avoiding vigorous thrusting. He should also protect his own back by bending at the knees when he lowers her to the ground, and again when he lifts her back up to face him. The couple can continue lovemaking with her arms around his neck.

1 First the woman lies flat on the ground with her feet in line with her hips. She brings her arms up and over her head to place her hands as flat as she can on the floor by her ears. Her fingers should point towards her toes.

2 She inhales and arches her back to lift her hips high off the floor, dropping her head back in line with her arms. This is the Wheel position. The man kneels inside her legs on his left knee. His right foot is flat on the ground and his right leg bent at a right angle at the knee.

# On polygamy

The status of a wife in ancient India was poor. Vatsyayana declares that a man is justified in taking another wife if his first wife is ill-tempered, if she produces no children, or only daughters, or merely if he has a roving eye. For this reason, he advises the wife to work very hard to secure the heart of her husband. But if a second wife is chosen despite all her efforts, the first wife has to become even more subservient, biting back her jealousy and giving the new wife pride of place. She should even help the bride to adorn herself in front of their husband, and show her every kindness and attention. But if a third wife appears, the elder wife attains a position of some power. Having befriended wife number two, she can instigate quarrels between her and the new favourite, which will hopefully turn her husband against both of them. Everywhere in the Kama Sutra the message about bad feelings is the same: don't express them openly, but if you get the chance to be devious, your revenge will be all the sweeter!

A wife who is disliked by her husband and his other wives is in an unenviable position. Her route back to favour lies in befriending the favourite wife, teaching her all she knows and looking after her children as if they were her own. She can also take on religious duties and lead in vows and fasts, endearing herself by doing jobs no one else wants to do. She can reconcile quarrelling wives and become her husband's confidante, procuring him secret meetings with other women. In this way she regains his affection.

3 The man holds his partner round the waist to support the small of her back. When she feels comfortable and ready, he lifts her off the ground, bending his knees to protect his own back from the strain of her weight. She wraps her right leg around him, keeping her left foot on the ground for support. He can now gently enter her.

4 When the man is standing firmly with straight legs, and can support her weight with his hands under her waist, the woman lifts her left foot off the ground and wraps both her legs round his back. In this highly sensitive position the couple can move very gently against each other.

# Seduction

The way to charm a woman, says Vatsyayana, is with romantic conversation. The citizen is advised to show 'an increased liking for the new foliage of trees and such things'. If his sweet words fall on deaf ears, he is advised to give the object of his desire some intoxicating substance, carry her off and enjoy her before she has time to come round, then immediately set up the marriage ceremony. Neither should he be afraid of going to even greater lengths. Vatsyayana advises his student to ambush the reluctant woman of his dreams while she is walking in the garden. He should attack and kill her guards, then carry her off and proceed as before.

A married woman needs a different approach. Poetic talk of budding leaves will be wasted here. Instead, the citizen should adopt the discreet language of amorous signs: pull on his moustache, make a clicking sound with his fingernails, cause his ornaments to tinkle and bite his lower lip. His object in seducing a married woman may not be lust after all, but a burning desire to injure her husband. Once she has been won over, the husband can safely be killed and robbed of his money and possessions.

**Above:** When the lovers are ready for more vigorous thrusting, the man can lift his partner up, supporting her back and bending his knees, so that she is sitting upright with her legs clasped behind his back and her arms around his neck. From this position, she can lower her feet to the ground to come out of the love pose.

# Cocoon

This close embrace can lead quite naturally into Butterfly, page 76.

**1** The man kneels on the bed on both knees, squatting comfortably on his heels. The woman sits astride his lap with her feet on the bed behind him and they kiss and caress each other.

**2** The man embraces his partner closely, wrapping his arms lovingly round her back. She lifts her feet off the ground and leans back into his embrace, raising her legs as high as she can for the deepest possible angle of penetration. The man rocks her gently back and forth.

# How a poor girl can win a good husband

**Above:** The calmness of the lovers' expressions and the cosy warmth of their embrace shows that this pose is meant to give gentle comfort.

A girl who comes from a poor family or who has been orphaned may wish to arrange her own marriage. If she can't find a strong, good looking man to be her husband, she would do well, says Vatsyayana, to pick one with a weak mind, whom she can persuade to act in defiance of his parents. Having selected her target, she should study his habits so she can bump into him at every opportunity, and also use her mother and her female friends as go-betweens. When she gets her beloved alone in a private place, she can give him flowers, betel nut leaves and perfumes. She can also demonstrate her skills in the delightful arts of scratching him and pressing him with her nails, and in shampooing (massaging) his body. Flirtatious talk is the order of the day, so she asks him coquettishly how he would go about winning the heart of a pretty girl.

While pretending to hold back, the girl nevertheless lets her beloved take certain liberties. She acts as though she doesn't understand his motives, but allows him to kiss her, and when he begs to have sex, she protests, but eventually and with a great deal of feigned resistance allows him to touch her private parts. When she is thoroughly convinced that he will never leave her, she gives herself to him on the understanding that they will be married quickly afterwards. Scented grasses and fire are brought immediately from the house of a Brahman and the couple exchange vows.

# Butterfly

The potential for movement in the Butterfly position is limited, but this is more than made up for by the intense genital pressure, which makes contractions of the pelvic muscles more strongly felt. The woman leans back to increase the pressure. The man has his right knee raised, which balances her weight and reduces strain on his back. From this position, the couple could move into the Wheel (p.70).

1 The man kneels on both knees, squatting on his heels with the balls of his feet on the ground. The woman sits astride his lap with her feet on the floor behind him and they kiss and caress each other.

2 When the moment is right, the man raises his right knee, putting his right foot flat on the floor in front of him. At the same time he lifts his partner with his right arm around her waist and his left hand on her shoulder. She supports her weight on both feet, leaning against his right leg as he enters her.

3 Now she lifts her right leg over his left upper arm and her left leg over his right upper arm. She leans back, clasping her arms round his neck, and he supports her weight against his leg and in his arms. The balance and tension of this pose are important to prevent damage to the man's back.

# Courting

When a man loves a girl he should sit next to her at parties and gatherings and take every opportunity to touch her. He places his foot on hers and touches each of her toes with his own, pressing the ends of her nails. If she lets him do this, he takes her foot in his hand and presses her toes with his fingers. If he is a visitor at her house and she is washing his feet, he squeezes one of her fingers between two of his toes, and whenever their eyes meet he looks significantly at her and with longing. When he is brought fragrant water for rinsing his mouth, he sprinkles it on his beloved instead. As she begins to fall in love with him, he craftily pretends illness and begs her to come to his house. There she finds him lounging on a couch in a darkened room and he presses her cool hand on his forehead, moaning that only she can prepare the medicine that will cure him. He then persuades her to tend him with herbal remedies for three days and three nights, during which time he talks softly to her, letting her into the secrets of his heart. Vatsyayana notes that though a man loves a woman ever so much, he will never be able to win her over without a great deal of talk.

**Left:** A perfect way to enjoy a radiant afternoon. The majestic panorama and gilded weapons tell of wealth and power. The prince and his consort have no need to hide themselves from the world because they own all they can see.

# Sultan

In this position the woman is in control – the man is both vulnerable and totally pampered, lying back on cushions with his legs in the air, while she clasps him and bounces gently up and down. Or she can decide to be motionless, gazing into her lover's eyes and using her pelvic floor muscles to alternately grip and release his lingam. Make sure the man's back is comfortable, as the woman is holding on to him to keep her balance, not to support him.

1 The woman sits upright on the bed with her knees pointing outwards and the soles of her feet pointing towards each other in front of her. The man sits inside her legs, with his legs over hers and the soles of his feet together behind her back. He clasps her around the shoulder and she embraces his waist. She puts her feet flat on the bed to support herself. In this position the couple can kiss and arouse each other.

# Heaven
# and Earth

Before the beginning was chaos, an ocean of menstrual blood raging in the swollen womb of the goddess Kali. Out of her cosmic period pain, Kali created the universe in the form of an egg. It rose to the surface of the primeval waters of birth then split in two: the top half blazed sun-gold and became the heavens, the bottom half shimmered moon-silver and was the Earth.

Ever since the split of the Cosmic Egg and the birth of the world, there has been polarity and attraction and a desire for opposites to fuse in a union of everlasting orgasmic bliss. This desire is the creative force, the sexual energy that dwells in all living things. In many ancient cultures, the creative force was represented by a spiral, a movement that can rise and expand infinitely, as it can fall and dwindle, without ever changing. The symbol of both the orgasmic clitoris and the horn of plenty, the spiral stands for the repetitive rhythm of life. The 20th-century discovery of the double helix of DNA, the genetic material that holds the code of life, would not have surprised the ancients.

2 The man now puts his arms back to lower himself among the cushions, and when he is comfortable, he lifts first his right leg and then his left over his partner's shoulders and rests his ankles at either side of her neck. She clasps her lover to her, with her arms over his uplifted legs.

The woman brings her feet back towards her, and plants them flat on the bed so she is squatting on her haunches. When they are both aroused, she guides his lingam inside her yoni, pressing down on the floor with her feet and lifting her buttocks to receive him.

# Woman on top

When Kali and Shiva join in sexual union, Shiva is often seen in the corpse pose, while Kali takes the energetic role, squatting on top of him, bouncing energetically on his cosmic phallus. This was the ideal of maithuna, where Kali took her orgasmic pleasure while Shiva controlled and reserved his own, thus recharging his powers from her sexual energy.

This position was forbidden by the patriarchs, who didn't like the idea of a woman on top. According to Hebrew mythology, the first woman was not Eve but Lilith, and God created her in the same moment that he created Adam, by breathing life into a lump of clay. God told the couple to go forth and multiply, and Lilith responded enthusiastically, jumping on top of Adam like Kali did with Shiva. But Adam didn't like it. The first man was also the first male chauvinist, and he insisted that Lilith, as a subordinate woman, should lie underneath him. Lilith argued logically that she was his equal and could have sex any way she wanted. Frustrated, she used her magical powers to fly away to the desert, where she made love imaginatively with many spirit beings.

Adam was upset and complained to God that he had lost his companion, so God created Eve out of one of his ribs. And Eve was subservient, because she came afterwards. But Lilith heard about this and returned as a serpent to tempt her sister with the fruit of knowledge. Everyone knows what happened next, but no one has ever been clear what the original sin was. Perhaps God had forgotten his command to multiply, or that he had given the humans sexual organs with which to do it.

**Above:** The sultan lies back, sipping a delicious cordial from a silver goblet, and abandons himself to the attentions of his consort. Note how Indian lovers of both sexes removed all body hair – for hygiene, aesthetics, and greater skin-to-skin feel.

# Antelope

Antelope provides the woman with a gracefully seductive sequence of sliding movements against her partner's body; she will benefit from the strength and suppleness that comes with yoga training. She needs to trust that her partner will support her weight as she lifts off into his arms, and he should protect his back at moments of strain by bending his legs at the knee. This is not the easiest pose, but practice will develop a fluid dance-like style that has its own excitement.

2 The man stands slowly, supporting her around the back. She lifts both feet off the ground, clasping her legs behind his back.

1 The lovers stand facing each other with feet together. The man kneels at his partner's feet with his right knee on the ground and his left knee bent. He clasps her round the waist as she sits on his left thigh and puts her arms round his neck.

# Congress with the mouth

Eunuchs disguised as women specialized in performing oral sex – congress with the mouth – on their male customers. Many were employed in massage parlours. A homosexual eunuch giving a man a massage – or shampooing him, as it was called – would pay particular attention to his client's upper thighs and abdomen. If the man's lingam became erect, the eunuch pressed it between his hands, chiding his client for getting into such a state. If the man said nothing, the eunuch would proceed with congress of the mouth. But if the man ordered him to do it, he would protest, and pretend to give in only reluctantly.

Oral sex began with 'nominal congress' – holding the man's lingam in his hand and moving it about in his mouth. After each stage of the congress, the eunuch expressed a wish to stop, but would be told by the man to carry on, with increasing urgency. Stage two was to cover the end of the lingam with the fingers pressed together like the bud of a plant and lick and nibble the shaft. The next phase was to suck and nibble the head of the lingam, gradually taking more and more of it into the mouth in a deliciously vigorous action called 'sucking the mango'. Finally, the client could bear it no longer and asked for the finale, 'swallowing up'.

In many parts of India, oral sex was practised exclusively by men on men, but the liberal Vatsyayana was of the opinion that everyone should act according to their own inclinations. He describes how some men have servants employed to suck the mango, while friends do it among themselves. The women of the harem perform the acts of the mouth on one another's yonis, while for many heterosexual couples it provides the ultimate experience of bliss.

3 The man now bends forward to lower his partner in front of him. Clasping her firmly round her back, he lifts her on to his erect lingam, and she pushes against him with her legs to position herself comfortably. In this position both lovers are excited by the limited opportunity for movement.

4 Finally, the man lowers his partner to the ground, and she places her palms on the floor in front of his feet to support herself. In this position, the energy flows between them.

# On jealousy

When a woman is very much in love with a man, she can't bear to hear him talk of other women, especially not women he admires and might prefer to her. The worst insult is to be called another woman's name by mistake. If this happens, she becomes enraged, cries out, tosses her hair about, hits out at her lover, falls out of bed or off her chair, or flings her garlands and jewellery to the floor and hurls herself after them, beating the rug with her fists in a violent tantrum.

It is time for her lover to effect a reconciliation. He should pick her up and lay her gently on the bed. But she is not ready for soft words, and in her fury she grabs hold of his head and tries to rip out chunks of his hair, kicks him as hard as she can in the back or on his chest or head or any other available part of his body, then heads for the door. Now she has reached the limit of her anger. To leave the house would be considered unforgivable, so she sits in the doorway shedding tears of rage and despair. This prompts him to redouble his efforts to apologize and reassure, and when she judges that she has driven him far enough, she puts her arms around him, continuing to berate him, but showing him all the while that she wants to go to bed, where the quarrel is made up with the most passionate sex.

**Above:** The couple are oblivious of the rose gardens beneath the moody sky. Later they will walk there and breathe in the heady perfume as the first drops of monsoon rain begin to fall.

# Rajasthan

The miniature on p.89 shows two Europeans, a Portuguese naval officer and his lover, practising the tantric arts in Rajasthan in the latter half of the 17th century. Foreign visitors to India were often enthusiastic exponents of tantra, though sometimes their clumsy efforts caused amusement among local yogis. The sideways pose shown in the miniature is a comfortable one for beginners, who can achieve it easily from a sitting position. The sequence below demonstrates a more advanced version, showing how the pose can be greatly enhanced for lovers experienced in yoga.

**1** The man sits on the floor with his back straight and his legs stretched out in front of him. His partner sits sideways on his lap, with her right arm around his shoulder. Her legs are together, with feet pointing behind him. The couple gaze into each other's eyes as he embraces her lovingly.

# The elephant woman

The Kama Sutra calls the energetic female lover an elephant woman. When her partner has tired himself out with lovemaking and his desire remains unsatisfied, she encourages him to lie on his back so that she can take the more vigorous role. With flowers twisted into her loosely hanging hair and her smiles broken by hard breathing, she presses her lover's chest with her breasts. At first she is bashful and ashamed of her eagerness, but then she is overtaken by passion and performs her part with abandon.

The woman can perform any of the acts done by the man, and in addition, her specialities are 'the pair of tongs', 'the top' and 'the swing'. The pair of tongs is so named because the woman holds the lingam in her yoni, sucking it inside her and squeezing it tight for a long time. The top is a more difficult and acrobatic movement. With the lingam inside her yoni, she spins round on her lover's body like a top. The effect is almost impossible to imagine. Finally, in the swing, she rocks back and forward with his lingam inside her.

When she is tired, she touches his forehead with her own and rests in the tongs position until they are ready for the man to resume the energetic role. Vatsyayana cautions against the woman-on-top positions if she has her period, has recently given birth, or is too heavy for her partner to bear her weight.

2 The woman leans back, placing her left hand on his leg to support her weight. She curls her left leg around the man's waist and clasping her right ankle in her right hand, raises her leg gracefully in front of his face, bringing it down to rest on his right shoulder, with toe pointing skywards. The man places his right palm behind him to balance her movement.

3 Now the man draws his partner to him with his right arm around her waist and she places her left foot flat on the bed to support herself. This is the moment of entry. The woman puts her right arm around her lover's neck. This pose offers little opportunity for movement. Instead, the couple feel love energy flowing between them. Constant deep eye contact gives a powerful feeling of bliss.

**Above:** When in Rajasthan... tourists try love Indian-style, complete with exotic drinks, weaponry, and a view to write home about.

# Sex and violence

Vatsyayana was of the opinion that sexual intercourse could be compared to a quarrel and he saw no difference between sexual passion and violence. Though he recognized that beating each other up during lovemaking would be repugnant to some people, it may come as a surprise to the modern reader that for him, physical abuse was the norm. Both men and women would wear their bruises with pride, as sexual trophies. Any part of the body, including the head, breasts, back and groin, were fair game, and striking could be done with the flat of the hand, the back of the hand, and even the fist. Our author recommends a series of ritual sounds to accompany this unsavoury art. The one who administers the blows makes sounds like 'phut' – something falling into water, 'phat' – bamboo being split, 'plat', 'hin' and the roar of thunder. The victim makes appropriate weeping or cooing sounds, and may imitate the dove, cuckoo, bee, pigeon, parrot, duck, goose or quail. As passion accelerates, so the couple hit each other harder and faster to the end.

Vatsya reports that in some parts of the country, the people use instruments when striking each other. A wedge of wood is the preferred weapon for wounding the bosom, scissors are aimed at the head, a piercing instrument is used on the cheeks and pincers on the back and sides. Vatsya draws the line at these practices – he calls them barbarous and base. He points out that they have been known to cause fatalities. The King of the Panchalas killed the courtesan Madhavasena with a block of wood while they were having sex. King Shatakarni deprived Queen Malayavati of her life with a pair of scissors in the marital bed and Naradeva, hindered by his deformed hand, blinded a dancing girl with a piercing instrument. Hopefully these salutary tales spared the lives of some of his readers.

# The Abduction

The man needs strong leg muscles to carry away his beloved in this dramatic pose, which ends with her nestling among cushions, secure in his arms. If other means failed to win a bride, Vatsyayana recommended abduction. If the girl was a virgin, her lover would be prepared to wait days to gain her confidence before the union was consummated. If the woman was married, on the other hand, her suitor might have to take his life in his hands and murder her husband, before carrying her off into the woods, which is the story told in the sequence below.

1 The man stands tall, then lunges into the dramatic Warrior pose, bringing his left leg forward so it is bent at right angles at the knee, and leaving his right leg stretched far behind him. His right foot is at right angles to his body for extra grip and support, while his left foot points forwards. His arms are at his side. Balance is all important, and this simple move needs plenty of practice to achieve gracefully.

2 The woman, who has been standing nearby ready to meet her destiny, now places her right foot on his upper thigh and her left arm around his shoulders in an attitude of sexual acceptance. He gazes into her eyes, placing his left hand under her right knee and his right arm around her waist. She puts her arms around him in affirmation.

# On different ways of lying down

Couples should lie together, according to Vatsyayana, according to the fit of their genitals. For the tightest fit to accommodate small genitals on both sides, the woman lies on her back with her buttocks on a pillow. The man should apply oil to her yoni, to make entry easy. The next stage for slightly larger genitals is called the yawning position. The woman lies on her back and raises her thighs, bending her legs at the knees. She lowers her knees to the sides. This affords penetration that is both sharp and deep. In the position of the wife of Indra, the largest genitals are accommodated. The woman lies on her back with her buttocks raised, bringing her thighs up to her sides and folding her legs at the knees like a frog. As Vatsya notes, this position requires some practice.

3 Now with his help she swings her body round as though mounting a horse for the getaway. She sits astride his left leg, supporting herself on the ground with her left foot, and embracing her lover in her arms. She curls her right leg around him and he holds her back in both his hands.

Sometimes, the legs of both woman and man are stretched out straight. This can be done with the woman on her back or with the pair on their sides, facing each other. In this position, the woman can arch her groin towards her lover and clench her yoni tightly. This is called the pressing position. If she puts her upper thigh over that of her lover, this is the twining position. Holding his lingam forcibly inside her yoni by practised muscle control is called the mare's position. The woman can also lie on her back and raise her legs up vertically, clasping them round her lover's neck. From there, she can bring his torso down to lie upon her own. She can vary the sensation by stretching out one leg and not the other.

4 When they are perfectly balanced, she lifts her left leg off the ground and clasps it around his back. She should weigh only lightly on his leg as he maintains this powerful dynamic pose. He can enter her now.

5 In the final stage of Abduction, the man lowers his lover to the pile of cushions. It is crucial here to avoid back strain, so he should bear her weight on his leg as he lets her down, drawing up his right leg parallel with his left. Gripping her arms in his, he is in a position to rock backwards and forwards into her.

# More ways of lying together

Some tantric sages were of the opinion that difficult love poses were best practised in water. This might make the standing position easier, as where the pair support themselves leaning against a pillar. In a more difficult variation of this position, the man supports himself against a wall and the woman unites with him, sitting on his clasped hands and throwing her arms around his neck. Her thighs are bent up against her sides and she pushes against the wall with her feet, bouncing his lingam in and out of her yoni. This is called suspended congress.

Sometimes the woman stands on all fours and her lover mounts her like a bull. This is called the congress of the cow. If a man enjoys two women together, this is called united congress. If he's lucky enough to enjoy many women at once, it's called a herd of cows. This happens quite often when a man is smuggled into the king's harem. In some parts of India, marvels our author, it's common for one woman to share many men simultaneously – her husband and his friends. Vatsya finishes his treatise on different ways of congress with a brief mention of anal sex – apparently it was especially enjoyed by the people of the south.

*Above:* The prince has his way with the young girl he has brought back to his palace. When their union has been consummated he will call a Brahman priest to marry them in front of a holy fire.

# Starflower

The name of this pose comes from the calm elegant shapes the lovers' bodies make as they entwine and subside, like a flower unfolding. Starflower allows the couple to relax after an energetic session of lovemaking. It is a warm and intimate pose that also gives each person the space to remember and savour the sensations they have just shared. In this comforting position it is easy to drift off into a blissful sleep.

2 The woman sits diagonally on top of her partner with her knees up and her feet flat on the floor. Her left leg is threaded under his right leg. Like him, she leans back with her left arm and supports herself on the floor with her hand. Now he enters her. Their right arms cross, and they put their right hands on each other's right shoulder, gazing calmly into each other's eyes.

1 The man sits on the bed with his back straight and his legs stretched out in front of him. He brings his right knee up and puts his foot flat on the bed, level with his left knee. He leans back and puts his hands behind him to support himself.

# Choosing a wife

The reward for choosing a good wife is a lifetime of blessings, for she will give untarnished love, produce healthy offspring and draw good friends. Vatsyayana advises his student to look for a girl of his own social level. She should come from a good family that is well connected with many wealthy relations. She should also be beautiful, in excellent health and of a placid disposition. However, the number one requirement in a bride is virginity, which, given the liberal morals of ancient Indian society, must have been hard to find unless the bride was very young indeed. Therefore, a man is advised to choose a prepubescent girl.

Before he proceeds, he should assure himself that she has no concealed defects, such as a hook nose, upturned nostrils, male genitalia, crooked thighs, a projecting forehead, sweaty palms and feet, or a bald head. If she has been named after a star, a tree or a river she will bring him bad luck, and also if her name ends in 'r' or 'l'.

3 The lovers begin to lower themselves gently on to the bed, letting their hands run down each other's arms as they bend their left elbows and go down on their forearms. The woman slides both her legs out straight at either side of her partner's body.

Once he is satisfied that his choice is a good one, the prospective husband needs to enlist the help of his friends and relations. They will make it their business to get to know the girl's family and promote his superior candidacy as her husband, boasting of his fine ancestry and noble character, and at the same time denigrating those of his rivals. One of his friends should disguise himself as an astrologer and produce lucky omens and signs and favourable conjunctions of the planets to prove how fortunate the match is destined to be. Other friends can be employed to create jealous insecurity in the girl's mother, by suggesting that other women are scheming to have him marry their daughters. In this way, he will quickly settle the matter so that a date can be fixed for the wedding ceremony.

**4** As their hands part, the man stretches his right leg out to touch the woman's left side. The lovers gently twist their lower bodies towards each other and their upper bodies away, so they are both together and separate, joined, but each looking into his or her own individual world. The woman raises her arms above her head and clasps her hands in a sign of wholeness and satisfaction, while her partner rests his left hand calmly and lovingly on her leg.

*Above:* In a variation of this love pose, the young woman prepares to strike her lover with a flower. More violent forms of sado-masochism were used by the leisured classes of ancient India to release emotions stifled by an elaborate code of behaviour.

# The Venus of India

Hindu writers have left vivid descriptions of their ideal woman, the goddess personified. They called her Padma, meaning lotus, the symbol of the yoni. She was heavily built and voluptuous, with fine textured skin as light and yellowish as a mustard flower and a face as serene as a full moon. Her flesh was soft and abundant, falling in three deep folds across her belly. Her arms and legs were well rounded and dimpled. Padma's bright amber eyes shone with gentle shyness like a fawn's, and tilted upwards at the outer corners. Special mention was made of her clear red caruncles, the fleshy dots at the inner corners of the eyes, a beauty asset neglected in the West. She had a straight, elegant nose. The breasts of the goddess were – unsurprisingly – firm, full and round, with dusky, well-defined nipples. Her yoni resembled the lotus bud unfurling into its full beauty and her love juices were perfumed like a lily newly burst into flower.

Padma walked as gracefully as a swan glides across a mirror pond and her low musical voice reminded those who heard it of the sweet song of the kolika bird. Padma wore richly decorated garments of pure white, and adorned herself with fine jewels. She ate little and slept lightly. She was meant to be looked at and enjoyed, but to keep herself quiet and unobtrusive. Her main virtues were her loyalty, obedience, courtesy and respectfulness towards her husband, and her main pleasures lay in worshipping the gods and cultivating her mind in intellectual conversation with holy men.

# The Horse

The woman needs a flexible back to be entirely comfortable with this pose, which demands a certain amount of spine-twisting. The man should take care to be guided in the depth of his thrusting by the receptivity of the woman's yoni – the most comfortable final position for her is with head down resting on her arms and buttocks up, so her back is not hurt when she opens right up to her lover's vigorous enthusiasm.

1 The man kneels on the floor with his legs together, his buttocks on his heels and his toes and the balls of his feet on the floor. His partner kneels at his left, their sides touching, their arms around each other, his round her waist and hers round his head and shoulders.

2 She lunges her left knee over his thighs. He supports her round the waist with his left arm, and his right hand encircles her right thigh.

# The go-between

In cases where it's difficult to approach the object of your love or to ascertain her feelings, Vatsyayana reckons it's useful to employ a go-between. Thus a man who is in love with a married woman and unsure of how she will react to his proposal sends her a female servant of his whose job it is to wheedle her way into the woman's confidence and beguile her with flattery. The go-between whispers stories into the beloved's ear, telling her that a woman of her wit, beauty and good nature deserves far better than the husband she has, who is hardly worthy to be her servant. She will blacken the man's reputation, pointing out that he is dull, mean and untrustworthy. If he is a small man lacking in passion – a hare man – and his wife is a voluptuous woman and highly sexed – an elephant woman – the discrepancy between them will be noted in mock surprise. Once the ground has been prepared, the go-between introduces the subject of her master, praising him to the skies and announcing that he has fallen madly in love with her. On the following visits she brings presents from the man – ornamental figures cut from leaves, earrings and garlands of flowers concealing love letters.

A woman can also act as her own messenger, going herself to the man she desires and telling him that she made passionate love to him in a dream. She gives the man a sweet-smelling flower whose stalk bears the marks of her teeth and nails and says she knows that he has always been attracted to her. Then she asks him who is better looking, she or his wife? Vatsya recommends that such a woman should be met and interviewed by the man in complete privacy and secrecy.

3 In this position the lovers can kiss and the man can caress his partner's genitals.

4 They clasp right hands and he guides her arm over her head. She is now ready to lower herself on to the pillows.

5 Supporting her hips with both hands, the man now rises up on to his knees, sliding her further forwards into the cushions. In the Horse position, he can thrust more vigorously the more her pelvis is tilted towards him.

# When things start going wrong

**Above:** This colourful miniature shows the richness and symmetry of the sultan's pleasure garden. Tinkling fountains, shady pavilions and scented bowers were essential props in the art of seduction.

As part of his advice to courtesans, Vatsyayana lists eight ways of telling when a man is going off you. She should look out for changes in his temper and in the colour of his face. She will know something is wrong if he starts letting her down, or fobbing her off with extravagant promises he will never keep. Another sure sign is finding him whispering mysteriously to his entourage, or, worse still, to a servant who brings a private message from an unknown person.

As soon as the courtesan discovers that her lover's feelings towards her are changing, she should act swiftly to get hold of as much of his wealth as she can, even sending servants round to his house disguised as bailiffs to remove his most valuable possessions. Thus fortified, she can get rid of her lover before he ditches her. Vatsya recommends disagreeable behaviour to put him off.

The sage advises her to cut the man down to size by sneering at his opinions and his learning, and by speaking knowledgeably on topics he doesn't understand. She can criticize other men for faults and defects he knows he shares, or interrupt him when he is in the middle of telling a story, or roll her eyes at her servants and laugh when he tries to impress her. She can let him know most plainly that she is disenchanted with him by her behaviour in bed. She will refuse to let him kiss her mouth and neglect to press her body against his when he embraces her, pretending to be tired and lying as still as a log while he makes love. If he still persists in visiting her after this, she should throw him from her house. Then according to Vatsya, she will have carried out her duty as a courtesan, which is to enjoy a man for the good times and the rewards he gives her, then to take him for all he has and send him packing.

# Eternity

This position is so called because of its spiral shape. Renewing his pledge of love after an absence from home the man curls his body protectively over the woman's. This is an intimate, deeply penetrating pose that can be achieved quite simply. The lovers gaze forwards into the unknown, shielded from its terrors by their engagement with one another. She pushes against him with her feet, indicating separation; he hugs her to him with his arms in response.

1 The woman sits on the floor clasping her knees, thinking of her lover. In sadness at his absence she turns her body away from the door, bringing her knees down to her left side and supporting herself on the palms of her hands.

# How to cope with separation

If a man has to leave the country or is banished from it temporarily by the king, his mistress will want to express her love for him and her dread of their separation in the most urgent terms. First, says Vatsyayana, she should beg to accompany him on his journey. If this is not possible, she will fall into a swoon and declare that her only object in life is to be united with her lover and that she does not wish to live without him. She can remind him of the times her mother tried to come between them, when she threatened to kill herself by taking poison, starving to death, stabbing herself or tying a noose round her neck and jumping from the branch of a tree. If her plea fails and he is determined to leave without her, she should make him swear that he will return quickly.

While the man is away, his mistress pines and neglects herself, wearing no ornaments except lucky charms and giving up her daily routine of prayers and visits to acquaintances in favour of anxious waiting. If the time for his return passes without news of him, she should try every means of finding out the true date of his homecoming, including reading omens and portents, interpreting her dreams and consulting the configuration of the planets. If there are signs that some mishap has befallen her lover she should perform rites and sacrifices to appease the gods. When he finally does return home, his loving mistress will give thanks to the goddess and perform the worship in honour of the crow to her dead relations.

2 Her lover returns unexpectedly, kneels at her feet and begins to caress them. The woman, who has been weeping, fearing him dead, half-turns towards him.

**3** He moves slowly up her body, caressing her back to life, then embraces her left shoulder and kisses her mouth. She rolls over into the pillows and he enters her from behind, curling his body protectively over hers.

# How to make a man fall in love with you

The first thing is not to appear too eager, because, Vatsyayana says, men are apt to despise things that are too easily acquired. Instead of visiting the man she has set her sights on herself, a woman should employ her servants to discover his state of mind. She may send her jesters, masseurs and confidants to entertain and beguile him. When they return, she will question them closely to find out whether he is genuine or affected, capable of attachment or committed elsewhere, indifferent or hard-hearted, generous or mean. If she likes what she hears, she will invite the man to her house on the pretext of watching a battle between her fighting cocks, or a contest between her rams or quails, or to hear her starlings sing. Then, when he visits her, she can give him a well-chosen present, something especially designed to rouse his curiosity and inspire affection. Once she has his attention, she can captivate his imagination by telling him intriguing stories. To keep herself in his mind after the visit is over, she will send her female attendant to his house from time to time, to bring him witty and mischievous messages and small amusing gifts. In this way he will be won over.

When he first comes to her house as her lover, she will give him betel nuts to chew, wrapped in their own soothing aromatic leaves. She will put garlands of fresh flowers around his neck and offer to rub his body with perfumed ointments. During an entertaining conversation she can present him with small intimate gifts, suggesting that he gives her something of his own in return. Finally, when he is fully aroused to her charms she will demonstrate her knowledge of the Kama Sutra and show him her exquisite skill in the sexual arts.

**Above:** The citizen reassures his wife of his continued ardour after a long absence. She gazes sadly into her loneliness, but in a sigh of forgiveness and acceptance, lays her hand on his. Meanwhile, their bodies rejoice in togetherness.

# Frenzy

The Indian miniature that inspires this position (page 109) is a curious one. The calm, luxurious surroundings show nature getting on with its business as usual – flowers twining in the carpet and birds quite rightly oblivious to the naked lovers below. Though the lovers gaze serenely at one another, their clothes are discarded in a heap (compare this to the carefully arranged swords, fruits and cordial glasses in other pictures) and their internal turmoil is betrayed by the whirling of their legs. Hips, thighs, calves, ankles and feet just go berserk. The artist has been carried away by his own passion and nothing matches up. If you are supple, strong and practised in yoga, try this pose, and see where it takes you.

1 The man sits on the ground with his legs straight out in front of him and his back erect. The woman kneels astride his lap, close against him, her knees at his hips and her feet folded under at his knees. She has her hands round his waist; he clasps his behind her back. She rests her forehead lovingly on his brow. When the time is right, he can enter her.

2 The man continues to support her waist as the woman leans back to place her palms flat on the ground with her fingers pointing towards her partner. She lifts her left leg over his right shoulder.

# How a man likes to be treated

A man likes to be treated like a god. In a long chapter, Vatsyayana gives detailed instructions for flattering the male ego. He comes up with some ingenious ideas. A woman should send her servant to the man's house to fetch the flowers his gardener had arranged for him the day before, so she can take pleasure in what he has already enjoyed. The servant should also ask for any betel leaves and nuts that were prepared for him the day before, but which he has not yet chewed. A woman should always keep her lover's secrets and tell him her own. She should take care to hide her anger. She should express wonder at her lover's knowledge of sexual technique and never neglect him in bed, touching any parts of his body according to his wish and kissing and embracing him even when he is asleep. She should provide a perfect mirror for his emotions, looking at him anxiously when he is deep in thought, hating his enemies, being subdued when he is depressed, pretending jealousy of any woman he admires and appearing dismayed if the slightest accident should befall him, or even if she hears him sigh or yawn. The attentive woman is quick to say 'Live long' when her lover sneezes, but wisely remains silent when he appears intoxicated. If he is sick, she plunges herself into a kind of mourning, refusing to eat, wearing only her simplest clothes and rejecting her servants' offers to bring her perfume and jewels. Lastly, she should take his sins upon herself, offering to carry out vows and fasts he has committed himself to in atonement.

3 Now the man leans back, placing his palms on the ground below his shoulders. He pushes up on his arms to raise his hips and the woman arches her back to lift with him. Her legs open wider, but the right foot remains as a support on the ground.

4 She raises her left leg so that he can slip his right leg between her legs, crossing in front of her body and placing his foot at her right side.

5 The man draws his partner to him. They clasp each other, kissing and rocking in an urgent embrace.

# The king's day

When the king awakes late in the morning, the female attendants of his harem bring him flowers, scented ointments and rich robes chosen for him by his wives. In exchange he gives them presents, and returns the clothes he wore the previous day. By noon, the king is dressed in his finery and ornaments. He then visits his wives in turn, in their private rooms, and his concubines and dancing girls. After a short nap in the royal apartments, he receives the servants of the wives whose names have been put forward to spend that night with him. Each wife has sent an unguent marked with the seal of her ring, and her reasons for wishing to lie with the king. The king listens carefully, then makes his choice. The wife whom he chooses is informed and her servants bathe, groom, perfume and dress her for the night.

A king who has many wives should behave fairly to all of them, cautions Vatsyayana. If his harem is large — maybe running into thousands of women — he should try to satisfy several of them in one night, simultaneously if possible.

**Above:** Artistic licence shows an impossible tangling of limbs. Despite their frenzy, the lovers manage to lock each other's eyes in a steady sultry stare – true tantra.

# Jacaranda

The miniature on page 113 shows a wild scene. The woman's hair flies loose as she swoops over her lover's body in a passionate embrace. Their arms and legs entwine spontaneously and the man lies back among the pillows, his lingam erect, waiting for her to take him.

1 The woman sits on the floor with her back straight and her legs open. The man sits inside her legs with his legs over hers and his feet touching behind her. They embrace and kiss, and she closes her feet behind him. They can stay like this for a long while, fully aroused.

2 The woman slips her arms down to the small of the man's back and supports him as he lowers his torso to lie on a pile of pillows behind him.

# How to tell it's love

According to Vatsyayana there are ten symptoms of being in love, and they get more severe as the obsession progresses. At first there is attraction of the eye, then attachment of the mind. This is followed by thinking constantly about the beloved and tossing and turning at night in an agony of insomniac despair. At the fifth stage the lover's appetite disappears and his body begins to waste away. At the sixth he loses interest in all the things that previously gave him pleasure. At the seventh stage he becomes quite shameless in his behaviour, loitering in public places in the hope of catching a glimpse of his beloved and not caring who knows how desperate he feels. At the eighth stage the lover loses his mind completely and he begins to rant, calling out to his loved one in delirium. At the ninth he passes out in a faint and finally, consumed by his passion, stage ten arrives, his heart breaks and he dies.

3 He raises his legs, clasping his thighs and holding them open with his hands, and she leans forward over him, sliding her hands down and helping him support his thighs.

Hopefully before this drastic stage is reached, the beloved will have given him a sign that she returns his ardour. Vatsyayana gives a list of the ten ways in which a woman can show her love. These include calling out to him without being addressed first, showing herself to him in secret places, speaking haltingly and inarticulately and showing·him a face blooming with delight, while her fingers and toes are beaded with nervous sweat. The final five ways are all to do with how the woman shampoos his body. Shampoo is a Hindi word meaning to knead: suddenly the couple seem to have become intimate. As she massages his body, sighs and rests her cheek upon his thighs, surely even the most unselfconfident lover will have got the message.

4 Still leaning forward, the woman brings first one leg back, then the other, so she can kneel with her legs apart and her feet resting on her toes behind her. Then swooping forward over her lover and pressing his thighs against his torso, she guides his lingam into her yoni. This is a passionate and precarious position, and the woman must take care not to bounce too vigorously, or she will lose him.

**Above:** The sultan abandons himself to exquisite pleasure as his consort hovers tantalizingly above his erect lingam. She is at once his slave and the greedy goddess Kali.

# In the mood for love

The student of the Kama Sutra receives his beloved in the pleasure room, which is decorated with flowers and heady with perfume, in the company of his friends and servants. The woman enters, freshly bathed and scented, and wearing beautiful robes, jewellery and flowers. She sits at his left hand and he invites her to drink. Touching her hair and the knot of her garment, he embraces her gently while they talk and amuse one another by embarking on subjects not normally discussed in polite society. The assembled company play musical instruments, sing and drink, until the woman is overcome with love and desire. Then at a signal from the citizen, his friends and servants depart, taking with them gifts of flowers, ointments and betel leaves. The two are left alone to celebrate their passion.

When their lovemaking is over, the pair part with modesty and go separately to the washing room. After this they sit together and eat betel leaves to freshen their mouths, and the citizen rubs sandalwood oil into his lover's body. He gives her sweetmeats and feeds her a drink from his cup. Vatsyayana suggests a number of beverages that might be suitable for the occasion, including mango juice, sweetened lemon juice, sherbet, soup, gruel and meat extracts. Then the lovers retire to the terrace to enjoy the moonlight and continue their agreeable conversation. The woman lies with her head in the man's lap and he wraps a quilt around them both, then points out the stars to her, and shows her the constellations.

# Riding the Elephant

Indian lovers were nothing if not inventive. This position is ideal for an intimate session in a howdah, the ornate canopy that keeps the sun off the elephant rider. The rolling movement of the beast as it walks along transmits itself to the lovers, who make no voluntary movements themselves. The pose can be practised in the bedroom if no elephant is available.

1 The man kneels with knees apart and legs flat to the floor, his toes pointing straight out behind him. His back is erect. The woman sits facing him, astride his lap, with her knees in the air and her feet flat on the ground. The couple embrace. In this position they can kiss and arouse each other.

# A life of leisure

The charm of the Kama Sutra lies in the exotic evocation of a life dedicated to sensuality. The pleasure quarters of the ideal citizen comprised an inner room, to which his wives were confined, and an outer room with a soft bed covered with a clean white counterpane. There were pillows at either end of the bed, and above it a canopy decorated with garlands of flowers. The air was heady with rich perfumes. Beside the bed was a couch and next to that a low table on which were arranged fragrant ointments, pots of flowers and dishes of scented bark and seeds that were chewed to sweeten the breath. The habit of chewing mildly anaesthetic betel nuts, which produces an excess of pink saliva, necessitated the discreet presence of a spittoon. Also to hand were various trinkets and games: a box of ornaments, a lute hanging from a peg made of an elephant's tusk, a drawing board, story books, board games and dice for gambling.

Outside the playroom was a terrace that looked over a beautiful garden. On hot sultry nights the women of the harem would spread rugs and cushions under the stars and prepare to make love to a loud chorus of crickets and frogs. In the garden the citizen had installed relaxing water features, cages of singing birds, a bower covered in creepers and a workshop equipped for diversions such as carving and spinning. Rigged up here and there among the trees were various types of swing that moved up and down as well as back and forth. Swings were often used during lovemaking, particularly in scenes where the citizen entertained several of his wives at once.

2 The man supports the woman's waist in both hands as she guides his lingam inside her. They rest for a moment in this position, feeling waves of energy flow between them.

3 Now the woman gets into position for 'riding the elephant'. Her right arm circles her partner's left shoulder as she twists her body slightly to the right, his hands still supporting her waist. She curls her right leg behind the man's back and holds it tight against him. His right hand slides down her left leg to clasp her ankle. She supports herself with her left hand on his side. In this position her yoni is tight around his lingam. Small rocking movements prove very exciting, and the man exercises some control by moving his partner's right leg. For more control, he can move his left hand up under her right buttock.

# Kissing

The Kama Sutra recommends kissing the following body parts: the forehead, eyes, cheeks, throat, breasts, lips and the inside of the mouth. Intense passion may inflame the lover to move on to the joints of the thighs, the arms and the navel. At first, kissing involves the girl just brushing her lover's mouth with her lips. When she becomes less bashful, she may give a 'throbbing kiss', moving her lower lip against the lip her lover presses in between hers. But when she is aroused, she will shut her eyes, place her hands on her lover's hands and touch his lips with her tongue.

Flirtatious lovers play a kissing game to see which of them can get hold of the other's lips first. If the woman loses, she pretends to cry and protests that they must try again. If she loses a second time, she must take her revenge by getting hold of her lover's lower lip in her teeth and nipping it hard. Then she laughs to wake him up and derides him by rolling her eyes.

Vatsyayana devised a language of kissing. To kindle love, kiss your beloved while he is asleep. To show you are attracted to someone, kiss a child sitting on your lap in his presence. Or while he is watching, kiss a picture, image or figurine. A man can show his intention when he meets a woman in the theatre by kissing one of her fingers if she is standing, or one of her toes if she is sitting. To inflame his passion, a woman who is shampooing her lover's body can rest her face against his thigh as if she were sleepy, then kiss him there, or suck his big toe.

**Above:** This love pose is a tantric classic. Its key features are minimal movement and sustained eye contact. The lovers float into a realm of erotic transcendence where sensation merges with eternity.

# The Path of Life

For this pose, the woman needs a strong, flexible back, and yoga practice will help her achieve it. Once they are engaged, she twists her torso back round towards her lover, who lies behind her. Her hips remain pointing forwards, away from him. With their legs entwined, the lovers look as though they are running together along the path of life. It is unclear from the miniature on p.121 whether they are standing or sitting, but put this down to the artist's fevered imagination. The pose should not be attempted except when lying down.

1 The man lies on his right side on the bed with his right leg bent forwards in front of him and his left leg bent behind him, as if running. The woman lies on her back on top of his right leg. He has his right arm round her back. In this position he can caress her breasts and her yoni with his left hand. Then he clasps her right hand in his and she turns her face to kiss him, cupping his face in her left hand.

# The first time

The woman is lying on the bed. Appearing distracted by conversation, the man loosens her undergarments and when she protests, he overwhelms her with kisses. Now he touches her in various places. First he holds her hair and her chin so he can kiss her. Then he caresses her breasts, which, if it is their first time together, she will try to cover first with her own hands. Then he moves his hand between her thighs, which she may have clamped together. But as she becomes more aroused, her body relaxes and she closes her eyes. He can rub her yoni with his fingers, then slip his lingam inside her.

The different types of congress involve angling the lingam to the back or front of the yoni, holding the lingam in the hand and churning it round in the yoni, holding it still inside the yoni, which grips it tightly, and alternate short and long strokes, which involve bringing the lingam almost completely out of the yoni and ramming it swiftly home. Vigorous rhythmic thrusting, 'the sport of the sparrow', draws the lovemaking session to its climax.

2 When the time is right, she turns to her right so her back is towards him. She stretches her right leg back between his legs and tilts her torso forward, bowing her head to his right knee. In this position he can enter her.

**3** He draws her torso back up towards him with his right arm, and curls his right ankle under her left knee to anchor her leg to the bed. She brings her left arm up to caress his neck and turns her face towards his. He catches her right knee in his left hand and draws it backwards.

***Above:*** In another pose that would be impossible to achieve without breaking a leg, the artist depicts the lovers entwined on the path of life. Try your own variation lying down.

# The virgin bride

Vatsyayana recognizes that the seduction of a virgin bride is a delicate business – the girl is likely to be both young and terrified. He advises her husband to abstain from sexual intercourse for as many nights as necessary after the wedding to build up his bride's confidence, wooing her with musical entertainments, visits to her relations and gentle embraces, tactfully pressing against her the top half of his body only. Once she has relaxed into his arms, he can offer her betel nuts wrapped in betel nut leaves. When chewed, this will cause her mouth to tingle with a pleasant numbness. He should kneel at her feet to beg her to take them, then as he puts them into her mouth he should kiss her softly and gracefully without making any sound. Now he has symbolically entered her body, he can begin to ask her questions to enter her mind. She may pretend not to know the answers, or she may answer coquettishly through a female friend.

When the bride is eager for more, she will give him the garland or ointment that he has asked for, upon which he may caress her breasts. The night after that he can proceed to stroke her whole body, and when she is willing he will loosen her dress, and turning up her lower garment, rub the joints of her thighs. Once she is fully excited, the lover can move on to teach his bride the sexual arts, assuring her all the while of his love and faithfulness. Vatsyayana cautions his student never to force his embraces on his wife, or she will hate him; at the same time, he should not give in readily to all her wishes, but steer a masterful middle path.

# Ganges

A difficult pose to achieve, Ganges benefits from yoga practice to give the woman strong arms and a flexible back. The man is in control, but the unusually shallow angle of penetration in the final step means that movement is restricted. Balance and grace are the key here. If the woman tires, move back into stage three, where the man can support her weight more easily for a return to more vigorous lovemaking.

1 The woman stands erect, feet comfortably apart, arms by her sides. She raises her arms in salutation to the sun, moving them in a wide arc to meet over her head. Then, keeping her torso and arms in line, she bends at the waist and drops her palms to land flat on the ground between her feet. The man moves to stand behind her.

2 The man braces himself with his right leg slightly bent and his right foot forward just inside her right foot. Supporting her weight on her hands, the woman lifts her right foot off the ground and swings her leg up behind her. Her partner rests his right hand under her thigh and helps her lift her leg high until she can lean her shin against his chest, with her foot pointing upwards over his right shoulder.

# Serpent

The double spiral of energy that can be traced round the two halves of the Cosmic Egg was discovered again by the yogis in the energy that lies dormant at the base of the spine. They called this creative force Kundalini – Sanskrit for snake, the serpent of Kali – and they meditated until Kundalini uncoiled and rose in a spiral to awaken the nerve centres of the body. The first nerve centre is that of sexual awakening.

As sexuality demands its answer, so Kali created the god Shiva, who was both her son and her lover. The Tantric sages taught that a man can only realize divinity through sex with a woman because women are alive with more spiritual and sexual energy than men – they don't exhaust themselves in orgasm. But a man can gain sexual energy from the orgasm of his partner. This is why, in tantric sex, there is no thrusting or violent movement, which would trigger ejaculation and end it all. Instead there are slow, controlled and graceful movements and almost static poses. Sex can go on as long as the couple like. Combined with prolonged deep eye contact and freeing the mind in meditation, yogic sex poses produce an intense emotional and physical awareness, a brimful experience that with minimal movement – or even no movement at all – can send a woman spiralling into orgasm.

The god Shiva is credited with the invention of yoga, which means yoke. The Lord of Yoga created positions in which the body is wholly balanced and centred on itself and the serpent of Kundalini can rise. By using these positions in the sexual act, which represents the striving in the universe for balance, Shiva could yoke himself to the goddess, ensuring her orgasmic pleasure while controlling his own, and thereby filling himself with her sexual energy.

3 The woman now lifts her left foot off the floor and swings her leg back, repeating the action of her right leg so that she is standing on her hands. Her partner supports her thighs as her feet point upwards.

**4** The woman arches her back, pressing her yoni against him and resting her shoulder and cheek against a large cushion. As he supports her thighs and buttocks in his arms, she bends her knees, dropping her feet back towards her head. Leaning her torso against his right leg, she grasps his ankle with her left hand.

**Above:** The prince proves his strength, and his lover shows absolute faith that he can hold her. Beware of tiring in this position – the woman's neck is very vulnerable to injury.

# Vital statistics

**V**atsyayana classifies lovers according to two systems: genital size and intensity of passion. The male organ, the lingam, he groups into three sizes. Men with small lingams are called hares, those of average size are bulls and the most generously endowed are horses. The corresponding sizes for the female yoni are deer, mare and elephant. The best matches are those between same-sized lingams and yonis. Strength of desire is either small, middling or intense, and again, an equal match is the most favourable.

The sages of ancient India were unanimous in agreeing that women get most satisfaction from men who last longest, but they disagreed about whether women ejaculated or not. They noted that a man could not continue to make love after ejaculation, whereas a woman could go on indefinitely. Some said this was because she didn't ejaculate, others claimed that semen fell from her continually while she made love.

Vatsya says that the first time a man makes love with a woman, he will usually come quickly, then gradually gain more control. But it's the other way round for a woman, who grows more abandoned and orgasmic with time.

# Index

**Executive Editor** Jane McIntosh
**Project Editor** Trevor Davies
**Executive Art Editor** Leigh Jones
**Picture Research** Zoë Holtermann
**Production Controller** Viv Cracknell

**Models** Angela Langridge at Walpole Model Agency and Patrick Jones at Samantha Bond

**Acknowledgements in Source Order**

*Jacket credits:*
**AKG, London/**Jean-Louis Nou front cover bottom centre left, front cover bottom centre right.
**Bridgeman Art Library, London/New York/**Victoria & Albert Museum, London, UK front cover bottom right.
**Christie's Images Ltd/1983** front cover bottom left.
**Octopus Publishing Group Limited** front cover top, back cover, spine top.

*Inside credits:*
**AKG, London/**Jean-Louis Nou 10 Centre, 12, 18 Top, 22, 33 Bottom, 49, 73, 75, 81, 93, 105, 117, 195.
**Bridgeman Art Library, London/**New York/British Library, london, UK 24.
/Fitzwilliam Museum, University of Cambridge, UK 7 Top, 45 Top, 69, 77 Bottom, 85, 89, 97, 121, /Private Collection 6 Top, 27 Centre Right, 37, 41, 57, 61, 65, 109, 113, 125.
**Christie's Images Ltd/**1983 15, 20 Top.
**The Art Archive/**JFB 101, /Victoria and Albert Museum, London/ Eileen Tweedy 16, 28.
**Octopus Publishing Group Ltd.** 2, 4, 5, 6 left, 7 Bottom, 8–9, 10 Top, 11, 13 Top, 13 Centre Right, 14, 17 left, 17 right, 18 Bottom, 19, 20 Bottom, 21 Top, 21 Bottom, 23 Top Left, 23 Top Centre, 23 Top Right, 23 Bottom Right, 25 Top, 25 Centre, 25 Bottom, 26 Top, 26 Bottom, 27 Top, 29, 30–31, 32, 33 Centre Right, 34, 35, 36, 38 left, 38 right, 39, 40, 42 left, 42 right, 43, 44 left, 44 right, 45 Bottom, 46 left, 46 right, 47, 48 left, 48 right, 50 left, 50 right, 51, 52, 54 right, 55 Top, 56, 58 left, 58 Top Right, 58 Bottom Right, 59, 60, 62 left, 62 right, 63, 64 Top, 64 Bottom, 66, 67, 68, 70 left, 70 right, 71, 72, 74 left, 74 right, 74 Centre, 76 left, 76 right, 76 Centre, 77 Top, 78 left, 78 right, 79, 80 left, 80 right, 82 left, 82 right, 83, 84, 86 left, 86 right, 87, 88, 90 left, 90 right, 90 Bottom Centre, 91, 92 Top Left, 92 Top Centre, 92 Bottom, 94 left, 94 Top Right, 94 Bottom Right, 95, 96, 98 left, 98 right, 99, 100 Top Left, 100 Top Centre, 100 Bottom Right, 102, 103, 104, 106 left, 106 Top Right, 106 Bottom Right, 107 Top, 107 Bottom, 108 Top, 110 left, 110 right, 111, 112, 114, 115, 116, 118, 119, 120, 122 left, 122 right, 123, 124.
**Thames & Hudson Ltd/** Ajit Mookerjee Collection. From Sacred Sex published by Thames & Hudson Ltd, London, 1997 53.